WORDS BY_

C000137703

Poetry and prose by human beings

**Curated and edited by Sophie Mackenzie,
Bethany Gill and Noura Al-Maashōuq**

In partnership with Unicef Next Generation
All profits will be donated to Unicef UK's Children's Emergency Fund.

Introduction

Since the beginning of time, words have scattered themselves across stone, page and lips to express the human condition. Words are, and always have been, our single most powerful and personal medium - they tell stories right from the heart.

But we, like many others, live in a society where labels have been formed to dehumanise, or exalt, the humans behind them. Because of this, it is not often our words can be shared freely, without prejudice or scrutiny.

Try to read these words without preconceptions: Refugee. Rapper. Recovering Addict. Londoner. Foreigner. Migrant. Trans. Depressed. Homeless. Gay. Feminist. Activist. Artist. Actor. Womxn. Model. Lawyer. Journalist. Author. Sex Worker. Singer. Survivor...

Within the walls of this book, 138 humans share their words equally through raw and reactive poetry and prose. Humans usually subject to the labels above.

Words By proudly acts as an anthology of the stories of our time. Without prejudice. With honesty and pride.

Words By also believes that investing in children, and protecting them from danger, is paramount to building a better and more equal tomorrow. This book is in aid of Unicef UK. 100% of profits will be donated to their Children's Emergency Fund.

In an era trying to divide us, we stand united.

Sophie, Beth & Noura
Co-Founders of Words By

Follow us on: 📷 @wordsby__
Visit: wordsby.co.uk

By purchasing a copy of Words By, you are supporting the Children's Emergency Fund and helping Unicef reach children in danger – thank you.

WORDS BY ___

This page is for you to write some words for yourself or to share with a loved one. You are part of this movement.

WORDS

I'm still drowning

WORDS BY <u>Salah</u>

How can we tell you – O sea – that we are also drowning on the land?
They drowned but they stay with us
They walk among us
They will judge everyone's
Conscience in us
When we left them to die in the sea...

The Forgotten Child

WORDS BY Lateshia

I just want to learn my ABCs
But the shootings keep taking my education away from me
Will I ever learn to read? I wonder
Because my love for letters and numbers grow fonder and fonder
Will you threaten to shoot me too?
I promise you please, I'm not here to harm you
I just want to learn my ABCs

Yesterday I learned up to K
Then my friend Toule's life got taken away
I hid for a while
Cried familiar tears
Only to tread on with familiar fears

I hide in the dark scared and alone
Hoping that I find my way back home
Yesterday I learned up to six
Now I'm praying I stay alive to this crucifix
My memories of Boko Haram have scarred me forever
I just want to carry on with my childlike adventures

We stay in a place where they call us the Internally Displaced People
But that's only because the minds of the terrorists are cruel
    and ridiculed
And chased us away from the one place we thought was safe

I want my mum and I want my dad
I want shoes of my feet and rucksack on my back
Please just let us go back school
We promise you, we promise we won't break the rules
We just want to learn our ABCs

Dedicated to the runaway children of terrorist attacks all over the world.

Weird Times

WORDS BY <u>Sam</u>

February was weirdly warm for a while,
Everyone in British cities was hearing stories
of people being stabbed
for things they don't use fists for anymore.
Birds chirped manically thinking
spring had already come.

Friends were depressed,
everyone was stressed
and certain pregnancies I knew about
didn't seem to promise
much for the new future.

Meanwhile, musky techno-prophets
Ted-lectured on the future's techno-promise
and reckoned on its dystopian potentials.

Swept under the carpet of azure Mediterranean
1000s of lives were left to the memories of their loved ones.

There was a dead bumblebee on the staircase of my block.

We could click to support the petition
to limit time in extrajudicial detention
to just 28 days.

Hazy days in London.
My hayfever came earlier than ever this year.
A boy I was teaching got stabbed in both legs
in revenge for a video he'd snapchatted.
It was a few months since my friend had been found innocent
of assault charges and possession of offensive weapons.

British parliament squabbled over whether and how
to implement the result of a face-saving referendum
that had ended up with egg on faces
and smiles that cracked on smug mugs.
The deadline to get something decided was just a month away.
Not a lot was very clear about who was funding what
and who was in whose pocket
but some of the murky details were published.
In a bland bar,
a couple on a Tinder date
attempted to make small talk
and at a pop up market in South London
people ate pulled pork burgers
in brioche buns.

Then in March, a man who declared himself a warrior of the people
in the tradition of mission-filled crusaders
stretching back to 1189 AD,
sprayed up two mosques in Christchurch
and the lead tip of copper-washed steel core bullets
rammed into human bodies
and ended some 50 lives,
all in the aim of a centuries old prejudice,
stretching back in various forms,
at various intensities
to at least 1189.

We Refugees

WORDS BY Benjamin

I come from a musical place
Where they shoot me for my song
And my brother has been tortured
By my brother in my land.

I come from a beautiful place
Where they hate my shade of skin
They don't like the way I pray
And they ban free poetry.

I come from a beautiful place
Where girls cannot go to school
There you are told what to believe
And even young boys must grow beards.

I come from a great old forest
I think it is now a field
And the people I once knew
Are not there now.

We can all be refugees
Nobody is safe,
All it takes is a mad leader
Or no rain to bring forth food,
We can all be refugees
We can all be told to go,
We can be hated by someone
For being someone.

I come from a beautiful place
Where the valley floods each year
And each year the hurricane tells us
That we must keep moving on.

I come from an ancient place
All my family were born there
And I would like to go there
But I really want to live.

I come from a sunny, sandy place
Where tourists go to darken skin
And dealers like to sell guns there
I just can't tell you what's the price.

I am told I have no country now
I am told I am a lie
I am told that modern history books
May forget my name.

We can all be refugees
Sometimes it only takes a day,
Sometimes it only takes a handshake
Or a paper that is signed.
We all came from refugees
Nobody simply just appeared,
Nobody's here without a struggle,
And why should we live in fear
Of the weather or the troubles?
We all came here from somewhere.

Societal Flaws – Planted

WORDS BY Tyra

Birthed into a world of pain
and planted like a seed.
Education systems let us down -
from society, we feed.
Condition by a world of 'likes' -
We need to know there's more.
Bridging the gap that leaves us blind -
a movement we're all for.
And although intent is always there -
it's not as easy as it seems.
We're surrounded by unconscious minds,
but this is not,
a dream.

Sonnet X

WORDS BY Katie

Home has a single, vicious claw in me.
She knows I am a likely one to stray.
She sometimes makes believe to set me free
--then plucks me back, and begs of me to stay.
And so we fight: I say, love is not love
that strangles anything it cannot bind;
she tells me, then you have not loved enough:
love is a tyrant, miserable, and blind.
No one wins. Home is jealous and fretful;
she dreads and dreams that I am falling ill,
wishes it. Home fears I am forgetful,
and tries by force my wandering mind to still.
Home is the gaping, hungry hole we leave
and that is left in us, who cannot grieve.

the denial of jasmine and other crimes

WORDS BY Amalee

when art is crime
then poems deserve capital punishment
for their vivid dance
    that vicious dance
to rhythms we know nothing of

I guarded the aged pages smeared in
the elements of suspended years
        and hostile suns

criminal pages seared between
    hand and chest
like they contained the last map on earth
/ in fact it was the last map on earth /

I traced the words back to the lair
    where nostalgia waited
under velvet verses stitched in gold
        revealed rhymes
robbed out of existence

& as I inhaled the pages
of Mahmoud Darwish who said if cities were smells
    Damascus would be
the smell of jasmine and dried fruit
دمشق رائحة الياسمين والفواكة المجففة
I inhaled here
the stench of discarded hope

& every time a page opened
a wound opened
    like when Nizar Qabbani said in Damascus
souls speak of their civil rights to live amongst jasmine
أرواح للياسمين حقوقٌ في منازلنا
and a new scar was born

Sharp Edges

WORDS BY <u>Salma</u>

I talk about my sharp edges all the time and by that I mean
    this womanhood
is like bringing a knife to a gun fight.
That womanhood is a weapon most commonly used against us.
That although safety comes first, safety doesn't always come first
    for us and
so we're often full of hard metal and broken glass.

It wasn't always this way.
We came here round and soft, wet with our mothers' kisses.
But even mothers have sharp edges and sometimes bitterness
    is a family tree.
Sometimes you can't help but inherit all the sadness that ran in
    your mother's blood.
And her mother's blood.

So when he sits opposite me and tells me I have sharp edges
and I can be a little cold and a little hard and it's a little unnecessary
I laugh and cry all at once.
Laugh because it's funny he thinks we had a choice
Cry because I'm still grieving.
All I've ever wanted was to be soft.

But you can never go back and sharp girls know too much.

We know what it is to rip a scream from our throat, throw it up
    to the moon and
hope that he lets you go soon.
We know what it is to never make it to the door
even though your palms were full of keys ready to scratch at
    empty eyes.
How you don't always have the chance to say no before the
    yeses are pulled from between your legs.

We've spent too many nights whispering in shadows because a
man's anger is a lot like bringing a grenade to a knife fight.
Have you ever fallen asleep next to someone you were scared of?
It can really sharpen your sense as you learn how to sleep but
stay alert.

We've watched too many women do the heavy lifting.
Seen them carry homes on their back as they crossed borders and
boundary lines.
Watched how they became a home for whoever needed them most.
Sometimes a young boy but often a grown man.
Men really know how to make a home in you and they
don't always build for life. Sometimes it's just a summer.

I want to ask him how soft he can stay when the dogs are out
for the kill.
When the bells begin to ring and the buildings start to burn.
When the death toll rises. When the war drum is a steady beat.
When safety is a luxury only some can afford.

What I want to tell him is it's not always easy to stay soft when
you're living in flames
and we women have been burning for some time now.

The Gravedigger

WORDS BY Camilla

I drive the bulldozer forward
There are graves that must be done
In the morning we will need them,
Tonight, again the planes will come.

I cannot help but wonder
As I watch the soil disturbed
If tomorrow it will be me in there
If it's my children that will be interred.

The grass is green like my son's favourite shorts
The earth brown like my wife's eyes.
The white marks upon the pebbles bright
Like my daughter's sweetest smiles.

Their lives are not just numbers
You see in black and white.
You cannot read in newspapers
The screams I'll hear tonight.

As the shovel cracks the hard, cold ground
My heart is breaking too
For my children, a peaceful grave
Is all I can give to you.

Ripples on New Grass

WORDS BY Ruth

When all this is over, said the princess,
this bothersome growing up, I'll live with wild horses.
I want to race tumbleweed blowing down a canyon
in Wyoming, dip my muzzle in a mountain tarn.
I intend to learn the trails of Ishmael and Astarte
beyond blue ridges where no one can get me,
find a bird with a pearl inside, heavy as ten copper

coins,

track the luminous red wind that brings thunder
and go where ripples on new grass shimmer
in a hidden valley only I shall know.
I want to see autumn swarms of monarch butterflies,
saffron, primrose, honey-brown, blur sapphire skies
on their way to the Gulf: a gold skein
over the face of Ocean, calling all migrants home.

Home

WORDS BY Nikita

I remember
my first home
in white flowers
with yellow hearts
of pollen, their smell
and softness
under our
car tires
leaving.

Longing for the fruit of my ancestral garden

WORDS BY Simone

'Go home. You're not welcome here. Go home.'

Show me home,
this place which you shriek and shout of,
this place you shower in my face as you shove past me in the street.
Show me where my home is,
draw me home, paint me home,
where I used to safely play sticks and stones,
and double-dutch.
Where I used to braid my younger sister's hair,
soft and silky to touch.
Show me my motherland.

'Go back to your own country.'

Words ring around my head,
screeching like worn car brakes,
as they come to an abrupt stop.
My own country is lost,
roughly moulded by the master's hand,
branded by his globalisation,
like the burnt tyre marks permanently etched
on the tarmac.
It is foreign to me, like I am to you.

Wounded by imperialism and invasion,
the opposite of gentrification.
You came and disrupted, interrupted my land,
and colonised my home.
Battered from the bombs, bullets, bruises and incisions;
violence springs back.
Weak and fearful on decrepit legs,
shaking, my country tries to stand.
She tries to rise.
We fled, tearful,
as our home begins blindly swinging the gun,
artificial weapons displaced in our clutches
to fight back against those who cut us out.

Foreign objects in her hands,
evoke an intense sea of exasperation and nerves,
as she sends away the heads of all the mouths her fruitful,
ancestral gardens once fed.

My mother wakes me,
scared in the night, pleading with me to leave my bed.
Desperately dragging her children to safety,
security.
Stuffing clothes into a rucksack,
a few torn precious photographs and sentimental scraps,
begging us not to look back.

*"Don't ever look back. Don't cry. We can't go back. It's for the best.
    Please don't cry. I'm doing this for you, for all of you."*

'Go home! Go back to your own country!'

You curse at me,
as you bustle past,
wrapped up in first world problems,
self-absorbed in your western life,
as the stench of alcohol, politics and vote grabbing
    newspaper headlines,
on your breath,
is rife.

Home;
I shiver as the word is said,
as it brushes my ear and haunts the memories in my head.

Home;
I wish I could return;
if only it still existed,
if only you left us alone.

The Confessionals

WORDS BY <u>Michelle</u>

He hurt you
So now you feel broken
Flooding your bed every night
Floating in your very own ocean
Emotions
So hard to control
Trying to suppress it
Hoping the pain will go
I just want you to know
It won't last forever
One day you'll wake up
And realise you're doing better
You won't be that standard token
Of the young girl who's broken
You'll smile
You'll laugh
You'll trust again
Even though that's the hardest part
Only this time
               - You'll be smart

Under the bus

WORDS BY Taj

Two days under the bus
With a banana and a bottle of water
In the night, I crawled under
In the morning, feeling scared, I'm hearing the bus driver cleaning.
After two hours, the people came and the bus moves
It drives around and it stopped
The next morning, it moves again
Feeling really tired
I think I might die here.

Wanting the bus to stop so I can get off.

This is not the end.

Saplings

WORDS BY Versailles

The beginnings of change are often small,
like saplings sprouting from the seed.

When watered daily,
they grow slowly,
but grow they do despite their greed.

Habits formed mindfully
may take years to become established in a psyche
once filled with doubt and hate.

Still slowly they grow,
edging higher and higher,
towards a calm and peaceful state.

Man Enough

WORDS BY Fisky

I'd rather feel nothing, than this sadness
So I reach for a bottle and a gram for a makeshift bandage
But these wounds aren't the kind to be bandaged
Offers of help
An alien language
I know what it is to feel hopeless
But what's left to fear when you've faced the hopeless?
It's crap to have nothing
You wanna collapse
Feel trapped
Perhaps you plan a relapse
Go in circles until at square one you're back
The Never Ending Story
It's time to quit
I can see where it's going and every sequel's shit
No progress, swamped in sadness, Artax
Consumed by the nothing
Do we fail
Or carry on until we're strong enough to carry Falcor on our backs
So, I'm trying out abstinence
And finding myself in the lab since I can't find my way out
   this Labyrinth

I can't erase the things that I've seen in my days
I can't take back the things that I've been
There's no way
To replace the decisions and mistakes that I made
It's no movie
Can't go back and re-enact a scene again
Director's chair empty
There's no actors anywhere to play
Our parts, cameras off
They can't capture all we say
There's no script
Wish there was then I would know what to say
No credits roll
Screen fades to black
This fear of happiness is crippling

I'm sitting in hell
The stress is tripling
Delve
In the depths of introspection where I dwell
When I'm coming up again for air there's no way to tell
So I'm
Left to peruse with this bottle of booze
It's been so long since my life's had any kind of rules
They got flushed
Now I got trust and a whole host of issues
It's no excuse
I know I need to wipe away the blues
I'm spilling my soul and I can't clean it up with tissues

And I'll never ask for help
I can do it on my own
But now I'm having doubts as I'm sitting here all alone
Surround myself with isolation
Writing in the beginning was only to escape a hopeless situation
I nurtured it too much and it birthed an abomination
A mad doctor murdered by his very own creation
The reason I write became prison I can't escape from
The reason the mic's a lonely form of aspiration
It's hard to plan the future when you're stuck in the past
The present feels like the past
These moments moving so fast
I'm drowning in life
Ain't gonna make it to the raft
Start to lose my grasp, clasp, my last breath
I gasp
Glass half full
The empty half reminds of too much
Running from depression but it always seems to catch up
Have a down day they say
"Come on Fisky man it up"
I've been manning up since sixteen
Tell me... Is that man enough?

The Oracles Oath

WORDS BY Miss Yankey

Shoulders slumped.
Eye's to the floor.
Uncomfortable smile.
Conscious of flaws.
Critical,
Cynical,
Captious thoughts.

How to unlearn
All the lies I was taught?

I'm finding reason
Through rhymes,
But my moods
Change like seasons.

I'm low
Then I'm high,
In this quest
For my freedom.

I don't know why
But I keep feeding demons.
And maybe there's none,
But I'm looking for meaning.

They call it soul searching.
Well, I'm lost amongst ghosts.
But I swore I'd keep going,
Took the Oracle's oath.
So just know when I'm less
I'm still doing the most.
Laying demons to rest,
Paying pennies for boats.

Death showed up;
On a white horse he rode.
He kissed my right cheek

And then gave me a rose,
Which he took from the ashes,
As a symbol of hope.
I asked him to tell me
What I already know.
He smiled and he told me,
"It's time to let go."

So I did.
And I fell
Off the face of the Earth.

I was the sun
    And the rain,
        And the wind,
            And the dirt.

I was the light
    And the shadows;
        The love,
            And the hurt.

The question.
    The answer.
        The death
            And rebirth.

How far are you
Willing to travel?
How deep are you
Willing to go?
Are you willing to
Face all your demons?
Are you willing to
Work with your shadow?

You know a seed
Must be dropped
Into darkness,
Before it can
Grow into light.
And you can
Travel in search

Of your freedom,
But the truth
That you seek
Lays inside.

Ask of yourself
All the questions
You've always been
Too scared to ask.
Be guided by
Your intuition,
Don't be afraid
To follow your path.

You were constructed
For greatness.
Your body is literally
Made up of stars.
You were born of
Supernovas
So remember
Who you are.

Shoulders back,
        Eyes to the sky,
                Comfortable smile,
                        Consciously high,

Positive,
        Loving,
                Beautiful thoughts.

I finally unlearnt,
All the lies I was taught.

The trade-off

WORDS BY <u>Kashif</u>

This is the story,
Of every person who left home,
Because of war, enemies,
And the fear of death.

I miss
My home,
My family,
My friends.

I can't find happiness without them.
I can't find peace without them.
Only Allah knows what is in my heart.
No one else can feel its pain.

Life is and will be hard for me,
Always.

I have to live in a different culture,
Without loved ones.
I have to face the hardship of immigration,
With disbelievers.

I moved from country to country through the valleys of death.

And now,
I am,
And will always be,
A foreigner.

I have more facilities, better dress, money and safety...
I am alive.

But I can't find peace and love like my family.
And I fear, I never will.

Send Them Back

WORDS BY Ramla

I don't know their journey, I don't know their song
I don't know where they've been or where they've come from
Brown, white, Asian and black
All I hear, is send them back

To the African mothers who dare to try
To the African mothers who make it across
To the ones who sought better, no matter the cost
The ones who grow trees from the seeds of great loss

If you knew their journey, if you knew their song
If you took time to notice that they're not what's wrong
If you knew their heartache, if you felt their sorrow
You'd see that these families are Britain's tomorrow

To the African mothers with the world on their shoulders
To the African mothers who go unnoticed
The ones with thick accents, the ones with the clicks
The ones with the nappy hair, the ones with big lips

You are my role models, my inspiration
The very bricks I believe build this great nation
Even with whispers, your voices are loud
Of my colour, my story, my history, I'm proud

If you knew their journey, if you knew their song
You wouldn't dare judge them, you'd say they belong
If you knew their sacrifice or felt all their pain
You wouldn't send them back and make them live it again.

London Riots

WORDS BY Karrim

We were cuddled up
on the couch
watching BBC News 24
and searching Twitter
for live updates
all across the capital

It felt like London
might decay
into a chaotic mess
of burning buildings
smashed windows
violent muggings
and opportunistic looting

For those few hours
an uncompromising fear
swept across the country

London was falling apart
all around us

> but I can't recall
> ever feeling happier

Knife Sentence

WORDS BY <u>Mr Milise</u>

Have we ever stopped to ask that boy that carries a knife,
What he wants to do when he's older?
If his parents are still together and who his role models are?
'Cos I guarantee you he doesn't live next to a Doctor.
Instead he's more than likely to be riding with thugs,
And they're the ones in the community prescribing the drugs and
...Driving those cars.
And I wonder if... as a teenager,
He's watching how the *"Olders"* carry themselves and it's
    learned behaviour,
I wonder if, by the age of 12 he never had a father,
And why, at the age of 13 he had his first balaclava.
Was he ever scared? Is it that Mum doesn't care or is it just that
    she was never there?
Maybe she's out trying to provide for the family,
And by the time she gets back she feels tired and angry.
Are there arguments at home; is there a lack of affection?
Are the boys outside offering you protection?
From the *"Youts"* up the road in a different post code...
The reason why you always go the long way home!
So the *"Olders"* on the block become your bigger brothers,
Now it's almost like you're related to each other
...GANG Related!
Now we've got a Council Estate kid filled with hatred,
Who needs to be initiated, BEFORE he's fully affiliated,
Is that environment just making him numb-does,
He have a choice or is it safety in num-bers...
'Cos they're not MEANT to be your MENTORS,
That's what we need grown MEN for.
To lead by example and to nurture ambition,
To teach discipline to understand AND to listen,
And I apologise for generalising,
For coming across like I'm stereotyping,
But we all need to know we are marginalising,
A WHOLE generation when we criminalise them.
Who really wants to end up in prison or dying?
And the social networks make it ALL look exciting.
The way that gangs incite violence live online,

And it's followed with an advert to make sure we're still buying!
And I'm not about to blame this all on DRILL,
But THOUGHTS become WORDS and words become REAL,
So tell me there's not a vested interest in what's manifesting,
When all the kids can hear is *"I splashed him"* and *"I CHEF'D him,"*
"Dipped him" outside of his house and then left him.
For his MUM to find him...!?
Have you been to a funeral and heard a MOTHER crying...?
When her son's in the ground it sounds like SHE'S dying.
...It's been like this for years - wiping those tears and... printing
 those TEES!
Saying, *"Put the knife down"*
Blaming police!
Writing to our local MP's!
I've seen mums at knife crime rally's begging on their knees,
Like... *"They took MY SON, but make it stop please!!"*
And it's our responsibility, have you heard it takes a village to raise
 a child,
But we're losing our community, so they're left to run wild.
And this isn't the time for answers or excuses,
But the *"Youngers"* NEED to know there are consequences for
 their offences.
Justice WILL be served if you're caught or let go.
'Cos when you take a life...
 You forfeit your own!!

Well, I'm not nice at all

WORDS BY Anna

My body is a battlefield,
a treasurer of the unspeakable.

It is wired internationally,
but crimes occur unnoticed.

New families seek refuge under my arms,
colonies form underneath my belly.

My stomach has been trampled over a hundred times.

There are dry bloodstains on my shoulders,
fresh wound cuts on my elbow,
and my wrists are broken from pushing out of this two-by-four prison.

My flesh, a sentence
containing wars in one body.

They've left scars on my knees;
burn marks at the bottom of my feet.

Secret services hide behind my ears,
they tell me things no one wishes to hear.

Terrorists crawl in my hair
until violence breaks out across my face,
my eyes pools of mud,
dead bodies laid across my mouth,
my tongue, a gravestone for those without names.

My back is a dessert,
a dry landscape, filled with bombs and broken hope,
drones fly over my spine, marking their territory in shadows,
and I sleep at night

Amongst the cries of dying men,
women screaming for their loss,
children weeping over the cause.

Madness

WORDS BY Dizraeli

There's a madness in the world today
A billion fragments in a tidal wave
The wave crashes up the old Green Lanes
And everybody's eyes are barmy

Must hurry there's a frantic rush
Up in the cafes and the cancer bus
In seven minutes we turn back to dust
And everybody's eyes are barmy

Eyes are barmy and our backs are sprained
Muscles spasming in nasty ways
Faces glisten like we're cast in clay
Ah look at everybody's eyes

None of these signifiers answers us
Professor Sanake and Captain Crush
Lady Ladbrokes and the Abacus
Everybody's eyes are barmy

And it's a crash it's an emergency
It paints a long and livid purple scream
All up the turnpike to Bounders' Green
Ah look at everybody's eyes

A machine collapses at the hospital
A stack of polystyrene boxes falls
And out the panic room a monster crawls
Everybody's eyes are sick

So stop your scribbling and stay your pen
They're putting needles in the rain again
A planet governed by insane young men
And everybody's eyes are barmy...

Don't Look Down On Me

WORDS BY Danny

Please don't look down on me
But if you do, what do you see?
Someone who's down on his luck
And has no way, to get back up.

Crying out in the night
In the night, all my fears
I'm trying to hide
But you don't know me.

I may once have been a soldier
And held my head up high
Or maybe someone's father
Cos we're all someone's sons.

But remember, homelessness can happen to anyone
Young or old, rich or poor
Woman, or a man.
You can always end up, where I am.

So when you see, someone like me
Just think, of how
Your life could be.
And remember us, who have been there on the streets
Cos it could be you,
Or someone you knew.

2 Fuck poems from #Fuck45

WORDS BY <u>Inua</u>

Fuck / Borders

The travellers of woods and waters who left by foot and paddle / who formed horse and saddle / rudder and sail / forged steam and engine and reached the holy grail of flight / So instinctive was collective strive / to boldly go / and yet go further / they went off-world / travelled off planet

The forestspiritchild in them who saw no borders in the sky / the winged wondering wild within / is who we have ever been / In time we'll wake to see the lines / these thin countries we have drawn / as utter folly and call out why / and when / and who / and what the fuck

Fuck / Border Guards

Heavy-booted and uniformed / the armed who man the borders / of narrative and myth / who cast the war-torn and hungry / as vermin / will say he reached too far / dared dream broader than his country / than wings could carry / that chant of his / that song of light / was foreign / sounded like a battle cry / too much like jihad / Icarus' whole flight / was ill advised / the father should have known better / nothing can be done / nothing as he plunged

Letter from a Refugee

WORDS BY Muzoon

Some people call us the lost generation.
We are not lost.
We have not lost our love of learning.
We have not lost our dreams for our future.
We have not lost our hope.
Dear fellow Refugee,
I want you to know that life will get better.
It is not that long ago that me and my family were right where you
   are now.
Exhausted, scared, and not knowing what tomorrow will bring...
I was 14 years old and in my last month of grade 9 when the
   bombing started.
I loved my home,
It was such a happy place.
We had to leave everything behind and find somewhere new to
   start over.
I was so scared and didn't want to leave.
I know how you are feeling right now.
It may feel like everything is dark and hopeless,
But there is light ahead.
Look how much you have been through and you are still standing.
You are much stronger than you think.
Me and my family spent three years in a refugee camp, much
   like yours,
And it is there that I started learning again.
But in the camps, I saw many people, many girls, give up
   on education.
Many would never return to school.
I want to encourage you not to give up on your hopes and dreams
   for the future.
Do everything that you can to stay in school because an education
   will help you build that future.
With knowledge, we grow stronger.
You may feel that no one will ever hear your voice,
I want you to know that I hear you, and I am fighting for you and
   your right to an education.
One day, I hope to hear your stories

About how my fellow refugees became engineers, doctors,
    lawyers and teachers.
And how many returned to their homes, their countries – to build a
    new life,
One better than before.
Never stop learning,
And never stop dreaming.
Never lose hope.
Sincerely, Muzoon.

TYCOON

WORDS BY <u>Sophie</u>

The child watches a white television box in her room at home. It is dark, but nobody has remembered to put her to bed. She has been told to be quiet. Mummy is busy. Daddy is trying not to be sent to prison. But all the children at school say that is where he belongs.

Mummy's bedroom is across the hallway. It is very big. The room has lots of mirrors reflecting the child's faces and there are two steps up to a pink and gold bathroom. Its big bed has many pillows. Daddy, when he goes to bed, snores in the room down the hallway.

For now.

The child can hear Mummy in her bedroom, shuffling papers. There are lots of papers and they flap in her hands, quicker and quicker, with a sound that cannot be ignored. She does this often, worrying over what has been written or sent. It is cold in the child's bedroom. The curtains are not closed. The black outside is an open mouth. A branch scrapes the glass.

The child wants a hug.

She opens the door to Mummy's bedroom. But there is only empty inside. A wide horizon of bed. Lipstick and jewels and packets of pills on the dresser. And the moon, reflected back at itself, over and over again. To swallow? The child's toes press into deep, plush carpet.

She wriggles them.

Then that sound again, it has not stopped. It has always been there. She turns. It continues in the hallway, behind the child. There? There. Mummy is still shuffling her papers. But she is doing it in the tall, narrow cupboard. The cupboard where her fur coats hang.

The child listens from the other side. The sound is more frantic now, this flapping, this quick worrying over words. Words. Once, the child found a thick bundle of paper, carefully cut out, printed with many she didn't understand. TYCOON. Is that the same as baboon?

Mummy?

She opens the cupboard door. The noise is on the ground. It is caught under a pair of gold heels. The high ones that the child places her feet inside, measuring how much they have grown. One day, your feet will be big enough and you can wear these, Mummy has said.

But that's not going to be possible.

The noise is on the ground.
It is black and flapping.
It has wings.
The noisy wings, they beat a rhythm that is *escape, escape, escape*.

But there is no such thing. The gold is heavy. The fur cupboard a trap. The child drops, looking with a close eye. It lifts a gilded heel, the sole scuffed. The noise moves. It has bursting energy. It ups with a whoosh that swirls and rams and folds itself in half.

It only wants to be free.

But there is no other home.

The child raises its hands to its head, its hair, its eyes.
Then Mummy is here, hugging, her voice loud. What is it? What happened? Tell me. Everything's okay. It's okay. It's okay.

There.

The child points. The black thing with wings is high above their heads. It dances and dips and is stubbornly out of reach. The bat threatens. Unlucky? I don't know. Who brings doom? Not me. After many hours, it is caught, captured, evicted back into the night. Where will it go?

It must make another home.
Before long, we all must make
Another home.

Unanchored

WORDS BY <u>Nida</u>

What does it mean to be free?

Sometimes I wonder what it would be like,
to evaporate into the air,
transform into a molecule of oxygen and join the rush of wind,
as it enters my house through an open window,
flowing past me in a wave of ecstasy,
before rushing out again.

I wonder what it would be like to fly,
to feel the coolness of the breeze and the warmth of the sun at the
   same time.

But not just to *feel* the breeze,
to *be* the breeze,
leaving everyone I pass in a state of bliss.

I wonder what it would be like to feel my own self so fully,
my own little universe in my own tiny molecule,
but also, to be a part of something greater than myself,
the collective expanse of air that makes up our atmosphere.

I wonder what it would be like to fly through the world,
and go anywhere I wanted,
not rooted to any spot,
not bound by the limitations of geography
or the human body.

I wonder what it would feel like,
to own this world.

All my life I have felt unanchored,
adrift at sea,
and uncomfortable,
in a way that disturbed me when I was growing up.

The fact of the matter is,
I'm still growing up.

I used to spend each day,
trying to figure out why I felt this way,
why I couldn't feel at peace in the security of my family,
the walls of my house,
knowing that I was loved,
knowing that I was taken care of.

Why wasn't that enough for me?
Now I'm starting to think,
I was never actually meant to cling to anything so tightly in the
    first place.

I was meant to be free,
I just never understood how.

Why would I want to hold on so fiercely to things,
to relationships,
to moments,
to concepts of home,
that are all just constructs of my imagination,
none of them permanent?

No matter how precious they are to me,
I have no control over any of them.

In fact, I have no control over anything.

And that's why I need to learn to be okay,
with just being that free-floating molecule of air,
whether I'm lying stagnant on a hot summer's day,
or whipping about in a fevered frenzy,
or even being thrown from one side of the world to the other,
in what feels like a catastrophic storm.

I have no control over what happens in this world.

So why am I trying to grasp so fervently onto what are,
essentially,
clouds,
reassuring and ephemeral,
beautiful yet banal.

I need to learn to let go.

I need to learn to let go,
and just enjoy the ride.

Maybe then being unanchored will feel more like freedom.

I am larger than what my body allows me to be.
I am a force of nature, bursting at the seams,
as if I'm trying to get out,
not out of this world, mind you,
but, out of my body.

I've always known that there was something precious inside me –
inside all of us –
but for years, I hid it away like a dirty secret,
under all these layers of my own making,
and now that I'm trying to strip away those layers,
and tear down those walls,
that sparkling and buoyant Being is expanding inside of me.

It wants to grow larger than humanly possible.

It wants to bend reality and challenge the limits of my imagination.

It wants to break free,
as if this combination of body and mind is some kind of prison,
but it's not.

At least, it doesn't have to be.

It's only a prison if I allow it to be one.

It's meant to be a vessel that I borrowed for a short time,
which will help me experience what it's like to be human,
to experience pain and pleasure and everything in between,
the way only a human can.

But this growing being inside of me,
isn't quite content with this arrangement.

It wants to be free.
Of what, I'm not sure.

How can I be both a human of this world,

and a Being far harder to describe, from some other world,
at the same time?
One foot here and one foot there.

How can I be in two different places at once,
two different beings in one?

Please help me,
to be both human and spirit at the same time,
to find the balance to float freely between worlds,
as seamlessly as the wind blowing in and out of my window.

Please help me to unanchor myself from my limited understanding
  of the world,
and to be okay with it.

I long for the truth,
but I don't need to know it all,
at least not yet.

Please help me let my Being evolve as much as it can,
even if that means it grows larger than the confines of my body,
as enormous as the Earth itself,
as inexhaustible as the universe.

Who says I can only be a human who exists *inside* the universe?
Why can't I be something greater?
Something shiny yet invisible, full yet free, everywhere and
  nowhere at once,
with the universe inside of me?

time to get a Real Job

WORDS BY Mikala

time to get a *Real Job*, i guess,
i mean, the old one paid the bills, but made the bigots upset
so i'll hang up my pleasers and lingerie sets
and exchange them for blouses and a monthly cheque

7am alarm and a desk
work the cold 9-5 and *Live for the Weekend!*
and get a whole lot of shit but get paid way less
spend my life deciding between being happy or rent

or since the clubs will always exist
i can still keep my job, it's just way more dangerous
i'll be seen as a criminal for my cheek to resist
an ill-informed ban based on a backwards mindset

time to start over, i guess
and i'm faced with the choice of selling coffee or sex
i'm not keen on either, i miss the stage and my friends
but apparently i'm dirty so i'll clear out from my ends

it's weird that no one asked me about it
but sandra and brenda said i was being exploited
and they must've known better than anyone else did
just remind me what club they worked in again?

they must've been forced without consent
but at least it gives me hope that i can be a politician
because if those people make decisions and tell me what my work is
they must've experienced it all to get there.

oh, and i guess i'm a bad feminist
because i thought the point was to let women do as they wish
but it must be to brand every sex worker a sexist
god forbid they dare capitalise off of a desired 'sin'

so goodbye to my freedom of choice
and to 700 others who weren't allowed to use their voice
did what we could to have the stigma destroyed
but in the end it's better for us to be unemployed.

Don't touch my skin

WORDS BY Hayah

An introvert with an extroverted exterior. I thought covering myself would help me blend into the patterns of the curtains and the wallpaper, but people are still intrigued with how I decorate the walls of my home.

I have to answer the same questions daily, have strangers touching my skin freely. Clearly, these people never been to an art museum before. Photography of the art is not permitted but most importantly keep your hands to yourself, no touching of the art in this gallery is allowed.

People ask me if they hurt, I tell them tattoos are a reflection of life. There will be pain, but then you will heal and you are left with beauty. But you are more than your scars, more than your past, so look past my skin, I am more than this art. This art has helped me to love my body. No, I will never stop getting tattooed and yes, if I want to I will do my face too. No, I don't know how like when I'm 80 years old, but I'm guessing pretty damn cool because they come with stories and memories. These tattoos have lived and will die with me. These tattoos have been on my journey.

Inspired by Chetna

WORDS BY Dipal

They might lower your light.
They might extinguish your flame.
But remember,
We will always hold your hand.

And my sisters say

WORDS BY Kai-Isaiah

For Muhlaysia Booker and all of you.

And my sister says,
"This time it could be me,
next time it could be
someone else,
close to you."
And I remember how you
forget we all living under the
same sky,
forget that some of us cry
ourselves to sleep for what
happens to us beneath it.
I remember that we gotta be
close to you for you to care
about us,
whether tomorrow is our
utopia or our right.
Like we gotta get close to
you,
right up next to you.
Like we gotta forget that kills
us.
We gotta forget our
proximity to you is the
reason we dying.

And my sister stops
speaking,
like trynna summon the life
out of a lifeless destiny.
And someone replies to her,
"take your time baby"
and I want to reach into the
screen and find any way to
make the past,
something that don't creep
up so fast,

cos it don't care for the
future.
You want us to forget how
danger is sometimes sitting
right next to us.

It will never be a
transgression or wrong, to
live there,
in the past -
for the present don't want
you alive in its stomach.
Today I have the flu, so my
nose all blocked,
can't smell the fresh air but
it feels like someone took
someone else in the dusk of
it.
It feels right up close to me.
You forgot that kills us.

I never found a way to reach
into the screen.
I want to call all the black
trans womxn I know,
tell them the worst kinda
thieves are the ones who
take us from our own
bodies.
I cannot tell them there is
nothing to fear
I cannot tell them that fear
can be forgotten,
like names that turn in royal
red confetti,
like locking windows,
and doors and gates.

Tell them that sometimes I
wanna relive the past,
just to know the security of
us all being in it.

Sometimes I wanna be
without a mouthful of dead
names.
All I know is everything I am
and love dying,
so I forget how to live.

My sister opens her mouth
and nothing,
I don't know if she is trying
to speak,
or remembering what it is to
breathe,
and forgetting at the same
time.
My sister says *"This time, I*
can stand before you,
whereas the other scenarios
we are in mourning"
and I realise I have run out of
time to reach into the
screen.
I have run out of time for her
to be standing
that we are already
mourning.
That I watched the same
video in both scenarios and I
wish we all remained in the
past.

I realised I have run out of
time to forget we are born
into a new sky.
I will come and find you with
no more names in my full
mouth.
I will trace yours
everywhere it can be, and
have enough room to kiss
your forehead.
Enough of a hand, that is no
longer a fist so I can hold

onto yours
and tell you,
how sorry of this new sky,
this heaven,
that is no reward of dying
and no compensation for not
living.
That we will not forget you.
Whether you are close to us
or not.

Unicorn

WORDS BY <u>Anthony No Filter</u>

I often found myself shouting, screaming, wailing with my
   mouth closed
I couldn't defend myself from the offence I felt from the ignorance
   of my world
Scared of my own difference
I often felt silenced
Falling in line
I had to conform, I felt stripped whilst dressed in uniform

I often screamed with my mouth closed
I gave my walk, my mannerisms, I gave my clothes
A voice
To speak on my behalf
To voice my opinions without me having to scream

Can I be heard now?
Or do you already assume what I want to say?
My blackness has eclipsed my star from shining light on
   certain matters
People enjoy the sun and I was raised to never rain on
   anyone's parade
But I've cried raindrops that diffract my light into rainbow colours
But I never saw black in the rainbow
So I graffiti-ed on my walls
Scars to show you that I can no longer be boxed in
or silenced
I often screamed with my mouth close

Being different from the 'different' but...

Everyone is different
But too many of us feel pressured to be the same
Those who point out your differences are also different
But they hate on the way that you cannot be tamed
They are sheep
You are a lion
You are a stallion
You are growing horns on your head to pierce through the boxes

they put you in
You are a unicorn
You are a myth
You are a reminder that life should be celebrated
You are a gift
You have to show them that you are true
Show them that they cannot disbelieve or not accept you
For you matter
And you exist

I'm so sorry that you have to make your own safe spaces in places
    where there's already enough room
Sing your beautiful song to a world so out of tune
Teach cannibals to stop feasting on your difference
Whilst finding the strength to love yourself when they make it
    so easy for you to hate yourself for being different
They outnumber you
Trying to be the same
Ignoring their own difference
Diverting attention onto you who was brave enough to be different
They fear you
"How dare YOU be different?"
The world is miles behind your mind
If we learned to be tolerant, be loving and kind
Maybe this world could be different

What kind of millennial being would I be if I ignored the stardust
    settled on my walk of life, paved by the stars before me
This pride of mine is celestial
People are too clothed in sheep's wool that they've adopted
    earthly comforts
They fear those who reject man made archetypes
They call us extra-terrestrial

It's like Hollywood Boulevard the way I strut on these stars
I'm stepping on sacrifices, hard work, sweat, blood, tears, anguish,
    pain and hope
And my pride ignites the match passed on to me to shine my light
    and be me unapologetically
To live, laugh and love freely

I do it because I can
Because they couldn't

Because some can't
I do it because some will allow it... and I'm lucky
I do it because some won't allow it
That's fuckery
I do it because some still don't understand
I do it because if you hate me
God damn!
I will to teach you to love me
Because I am...

A unicorn
I am a 'myth'
I am the reason that life should be celebrated
I am a gift
I will show you that you cannot disbelieve or not accept me
For I exist
And I matter
And I will scream with every voice of every brave being who died
    giving birth to my pride
Because I often screamed with my mouth closed

How disrespectful of me

The Blind Side

WORDS BY Ingrid

As I look through the window, nothing has changed much.
Women shuffle around in unison with their eyes wide shut.
Behind steel desks sit stained smiles and strangulated stories,
You see, these are the classrooms where they're taught not to
  shine or magnitude their glory.
In the watchtowers are the guards who used to stop and strip
  search me regularly,
try to strip me of my individuality,
They'd say things like,
You're not black, because I don't say fam, I say family,
Or that,
Women like you, you have no identity,
Or that,
I'm no lady,
Because I speak my mind freely.
But as they strip me,
I sing...

Slaves jumped from ships
they had run to be free
they shed their blood
to create women like me

Every day more women captured and become even more afraid
  to switch,
For fear of being called a nasty woman or a witch,
On arrival they strip them of their superwoman capes,
and show them examples of those who have dared to escape,
They,
Single them out,
Ostracize them,
They burn them at the stake.

But at they burn me,
I sing...

Slaves jumped from ships
they had run to be free

they shed their blood
to create women like me

You see, back in those days women were silenced and treated
   like property,
That's right for over 400 years they enslaved up those before me,
and now you want me to come slave up my mind too like I'm some
   fucking wannabee,
NO, this big mouth,
THIS BIG MOUTH is to ensure that their souls don't die empty.
This is me, mother fuckers and I make no apology,
As I SING...

Slaves jumped from ships
they had run to be free
they shed their blood
to create women like me

Ssshhh,
Just then the window reveals a potential badass gal in the wings,
Now, I always have a nose for sniffing out those whose song inside
   them is bursting to sing,
And so I whisper to her,
Mother's we need to create a new philosophy,
before they rape our babies of their powers and badassery.
Before they're made to believe that what defines them are their
   boobs and behind,
Not their brains, their achievements or their magnificent minds,
For them to,
ditch the belief that their net worth is based on how boys and men
   rate them,
For them to have no fear of escaping from this factory that is clearly
   fucking killing them.
I mean you can see it too right???
By age six future leaders are amputated,
Injected with a vaccine of untruths about their awesomeness,
On the factory belt they stitch down their arms like penguins,
then stuff them into tiny boxes that are clearly too fucking small
   for them.
They remove their shiny shoes,
replace them with tiny pins,
paint on their smiles,
And stuff their souls into plastic mannequins

And so I sing...

Slaves jumped from ships
they had run to be free
they shed their blood
to create women like me

I'm not going to lie, this side of the wall can often feel so lonely,
I have often wondered if I'd be better off in the factory because at
    least I'd have company,
but just as I was about to have that ugly thought once more,
I hear about some art form called spoken word poetry.
Now I'm here rocking with fellow warriors who've used their pens
    like swords to escape the factory,
Women and men,
Running free,
Stepping into their power,
and being the badasses
That they were born to be,
As WE sing...

Slaves jumped from ships
they had run to be free
they shed their blood
But not in vain
because now there are women and men like YOU
and like me.

Garden of Eden

WORDS BY The Nasty Poet

Here it is,
Love unfreed,
Peeled back,
A battlefield.

Field of gold,
Moulding green,
Copper sold.

Bought a dud thing.

Green stains on my fingers,
Fake smile,
Pruning for a while.

The Garden of Eden,
Lies in ruins,
Live in rage,
Living wage,
Burning sage.

I've not lived in an age.

Gardeners in the sky,
I've been trying to keep the grass alive,
I'd not grass you, if you were the last to survive,
You'll pass yourself up,
I won't even have tried.

I'm tired of raking the leaves,
That autumn breathes.

Should have saved,
Autumn braved,
The fall that should have came.

Seasons down,
And I'll be seasons out,

Undercover.
To recover.

I'd slight,
And you'd gas light.
Shut Up,
And turn the lights out.

From the throat down,
I'd choke down,
That feeling,
Just to feel again.

Darker out,
Darkness descends down.
It never lifted.
You could lift me.

Could pull right,
I'm still living in the dull light.
Summer's here,
And I play in the shadows.

Now I bow down,
Hands together.
Hoping to see the sun down,
Set in the Garden of Eden again.

Injustices

WORDS BY Tash

This justice system – it's disgusting.
NEWS JUST IN
Lawful killings are not hidden.
Nor the over representation of black males in prison, while
Crime is ridden through all races
Places, and innocent faces,

And when they criminalise
Us.
They're not trying to save us.
Nor to change the prearranged, just
Shame.
Tame.
Contain those wilder flames
As they warm their fat feet on the fire that fuels their immunity.
Who even are they?
You'll find those who monopolise this game,
Sitting in peace,
First class reserved seat on a Virgin again,

Aging frame,
Holding tight their pride of a titanium name
And there they stay...

Because they know they'll see pain when they come to the back
    of the train
Now I'm not saying for one second,
That any man
Should not be thriving.
But there are differences in the conditions we're expected to
    survive in,
Some mothers suffering whilst other piggy hands just dive in
And before I talk of personal experience,
Let me widen the horizons
Because we are living in a world
Where the top 10 leading causes of death
Are diseases of excess
From too much stress and a lifetime of saying

I should have drunk less.
Symptoms of the West
Heart attack
Stroke
Diabetes
Alzheimers.

They happen to happen to loved characters
Legendary old timers
Who had a long life and beautiful wife before the nephritis set in,
And then after a while, they just

Let in the idea of death.
Knowing they'll leave smiles past their very last breath.

Number 10 is suicide.
Bless them.
For committing to valuing the absence of life's lessons.
They came.
They did their time.

And it's mad that suicide is even a crime because some of us are
    given hills that are just too steep to climb and never got a leg up.

But
Much,
Much,
Lower
Down on this list, is a problem that shouldn't still fucking exist.

As I say this I clench my fist
I urge you to do the same.
Do it.

Now look at it.

Because this is the size of your stomach.

There just is.
More than enough food to feed every hungry person on this
    earth but there is not nearly enough compassion, responsibility,
    or organisation to enable the statistically few to cease making
    choices like -

Do I feed my infant dirty water today?
Or nothing,
And pray,
Oh child! I'm sorry I brought you into this place,
But currently the currency of our skin, its worthless,
Political waste.
It didn't always used to be this way
It just is, right now, okay?
I'm sorry you'll never grow to have an old man's face,
Or even know enough substance to get off it,
To make mistakes,
The thing about this world child,
Is we tend to stay in our allocated spaces.

And I'm sorry it's us who wake up to mass graves.

We all know, that the law has abolished slaves.
But how much are we getting paid
To ignore the screams of those being crushed at the bottom
While we're airlifted to somewhere safe?

مبدأ الحياء .. من يحاول أن يخسر ساعده

منذ يوم ولادتي نظرت في عينيك وشعرت بحبك الحلو.

كنت أعرف أنك أنت عندما أفتح عيني
ونسمع من أعلاه سأكون هناك عندما تطير
سأكون هناك عندما تهبط سأكون هناك عندما تكون خارج المنزل
فراشتي.
ليس الحب وحده بل الإحساس (للسؤولية عن روح أخرى تسكن روحك

لقد تعبت من الحزن وأحتاج إلى الترحيب الحار.

كل شيء سيكون صحيحًا إذا بدأت في اتخاذ الخطوات الصحيحة لذلك.
ليس الحب مجرد فحسب بل هون شعورك بالسؤولية عن روح أخرئ تسكن روحك.
أني تعبت من الحزن واحتاج ألحضه أرتاح يا صاحي راح المن حبيي راححج..
كل شيء سيكون صحيحًا إذا اتخذت الخطوات الصحيحة عليه..
بيع بيع.. ولا تضن بعدك أضيع أني متهزني الجراح الان ماحب المتاح الجميع!!

ليس الحب مجرد فحسب بل هو شعورك بالسؤولية عن روح أخرى تسكن روحك.
اني تعبت من الحزن و احتاج الحضه أرتاح يا صاحي راح الفرح المن حبيي راحج.

The Stories That Change You

WORDS BY <u>Catrin</u>

Last week I interviewed a woman dying on sofa in a rented flat in a London suburb because she doesn't have the right visa to be cared for.

She was calm as she told me her story. Pragmatic as she explained that this wasn't the way she thought her final days would be. Possibly calmer than me – my voice cracked slightly as I asked her questions about her diagnosis.

I'm a journalist. We are used to hearing heartbreak and suffering, and the job requires you to be cool and calm when at work. Save being upset for after the interview if you need to. And anyway: how dare I feel sad when it's them suffering, not me?

But even so, some stories stay with you, they change you. Almost five years ago I reported on the life, kidnap and brutal murder by Isis terrorists of a British taxi driver that we all called 'Gadget'. His full name was Alan Henning. I had met him and travelled on two aid convoys to Syria with his closest friends, who were with him when he was taken away. For weeks I spoke on TV and radio. I was a news reporter but I was also felt personally closer to this story than any I'd covered before. I had known about the kidnap for months before it was made public and had to keep quiet. Everyone was hoping there would be a happy ending.

But there was no happy ending. Alan Henning was beheaded in the desert, thousands of miles from home. It was filmed and plastered all over the internet. It still seems too horrific to be real.

The story of Gadget changed the journalism I've done since. It's why I work with the charity that's created this book. It took over my personal life because I struggled to think about anything else. Even now, it's somewhere in the back of mind. I've just returned from a hostile environment training course that all BBC journalists take before reporting in somewhere especially dangerous. We practiced what it's like to be kidnapped, being held in captive in a mocked up room. Was Gadget's room like this one, I wondered? Did he think he would leave? Did he really ask them for better coffee, as someone told me? What was he thinking on the day he died – did he know?

I'm just a reporter who knew him a little. For his children this isn't a news story, but the story of their father's death. Every day his family think of him and try and concentrate on the good he was trying to do for Syria. And I will think of him always too - because some stories stay.

Asiya's Story

WORDS BY <u>Conscious Rhymes</u>

Do you know the story of young Asiya?
A beautiful child, her eyes were bright enough,
To light the whole sky and illuminate her soul,
She had big dreams, big plans, big goals,
She could have been anything she put her mind to,
She was smart, intelligent, a child just like you,
Once were and as your children are now,
So I ask you, is this how,
She deserved to be treated, left and lost in a ditch?
Her mother was raped and her father had gone amiss,

Young Asiya sat with tears in her eyes,
Calling out to the skies to ask why,
As she looked up above, another drone flew by,
As it dropped its load she felt the earth sigh,

"Is this what we have lowered ourselves to?
The genocide of a nation for resources and fuel?
For power and authority in all matters?
For control of the people, humanity has been shattered."

Young Asiya was only nine years old,
She had a prosperous future to uphold,
Her favourite toy to toy with was her stethoscope,
Wanted to be a nurse to cure the sick,
May God bless her soul,

This innocent soul that didn't deserve this plight,
I can only look at her corpse and think about her life,
As she walked for three days to make it to the waters,
Only to find out there was a shortage,
Of boats to carry them all across safely,
In a desperate, hopeful search for safety,
She wormed her way through, like a mouse in a matrix,
She made it onto the boat, her saviour that would save this,
Innocent soul from the screams of her hometown,
But little did she know that boat would drown,
That vessel that claimed to be a saviour,
Would end up being her biggest failure,

Just like the system that failed her,
That promised to protect and to save her,
Just like the system that created the system,
The one that she ran to as though they would listen,
As though the ones who created the war,
Would invite into their homes the displaced and the poor,

You turned Asiya away and forced her back,
On the boat which had no space to breathe it was packed,
To the brim with all these refugees,
They hid their pain, only let you see,
That they were displaced, in dire need,
They were lost and came begging at your feet,
And you kicked them away, you kicked away young Asiya,
Under the guise of *"these bloody immigrants"* you laughed at her,

But all I feel is sorrow and pain,
For young Asiya who was turned away,
And forced to go back the way she came,
Back to the land from where she was forced away,

But as we know the boat never made it that far,
So where is justice for Asiya?
And the thousands of children, women and men like her,
Who were betrayed by their systems, abandoned and hurt,
Bloody and bruised, families dismembered,
And the media forgets this, none of them will be remembered,

So I paint Asiya's Story on my canvas for you,
I paint it with her blood so you can walk in her shoes,
Know that foreign policy has created this genocide,
So now you can sit back and watch your brothers and sisters die,
All whilst you allow the system to lie,
But where is Asiya's justice?
She was only nine!
Where is the system that will protect,
From the evil that continues to manifest,
But we know one day that victory is promised,
So I urge you all, for Asiya, to work for it.

So much war and genocide,
Paint for you by Conscious Rhymes.

War

WORDS BY <u>Khalil</u>

War.

Damascus, the oldest city in the *world*, seen by the *world*, and let
  me say these *words*;
Why me?
Why others?
Why Abel?

The first human to commit murder,
Has chosen it to happen in Damascus.
And here I am, dying?
My mother is calling, crying,
Knowing where I am,
Knowing bodies were flying.
Mum I am lucky,
Don't you worry.
Being in the underground has saved my life from flying.
Where I am sorry for those people who were above me dying.
It was just an explosion, the sun is shining,
and luckily, I am surviving.
Sixteen years old, escaping alone, dark sky, hope stars and
  cold water.
Crossing the land and sea,
Syrian with a German passport
Flying, landing and living.
To a safe spot... London.
I made it,
Can you make it?

I am a human,
Just like you,
Call me a refugee,
As long as I am breathing.
But let me tell you;
Death is coming, for me and you,
So be a good person and enjoy living.

Roast Potatoes and ISIS

WORDS BY <u>Sophie</u>

Roast potatoes and ISIS
Garden peas and crisis
It's a twisted form of Gogglebox
We all agree it's bad and we need politely
See that custard is really lovely
It's on the otherside of the world so it's got nothing to do with me
What's for pudding is it ice cream?
Yum yum yum Brexit is fucking up country

Mum calls for us and says, *"Dinners ready!"*
Back in the day when our heads were less heavy
And I'm eleven years old, uniform on, tucked in, napkin to my chin
My mum tuts at the way that the world is spinning and says,
  "We can't begin to imagine what it's like to be at war"
But we shouldn't concern ourselves too much because our brains
  are too small

Polite knives and forks placed at half past six
On the TV the Iraq War, confused as to who exactly caused it
But I try to comprehend it, how they seem to grin and bare it
Until I ask for more roast potatoes and garden peas
Because even now at twenty-two I don't really understand
  another land
I've been brought up to sit and watch and watch and eat
My brain gets numb, but I'll still feast
"Someone else can bother, try fix the Far East
It's on the otherside of the world, it's got nothing to do with me
Yum yum yum
I'll just turn off the TV"

Your Food Smells

WORDS BY Riaz

"Your Food Smells!"
"What's that funny bread?"
"Is it from Africa?"
"It looks like a sponge!"
"That looks like dog food"
"It SMELLS like dog food"
"Is it from Timbuktu?"
"It PONGS!"
"Why don't you just get school dinners?"

"Was that Hardo Bread?"
Yeah!
"and plantain?"
Yeah!
Curry Goat!
Yeah! you have this too?
"Yeah"
Bigga Fruit Punch!
"You know!"

They Don't Know

Body

WORDS BY Tannika

Confidence is key don't ever feel guilty about it,
I'm not responsible for what you see so I never feel guilty about it,
Who created all these so-called standards for us?
Where the big should be smaller and the small should be
   slightly bigger,
Anything less is a social disaster.

I'm proud to be imperfect because I'm perfect to me,
What's perfect to you isn't realistic for me,
I can't live a life based on what people want to see to
   achieve acceptance,
The acceptance from people that can't embrace difference,
Life has shown us that beauty opens doors,
And there's nothing wrong with that,
But don't undermine your own because you don't fit in with that.

Rejections aren't confirmation of your imperfections,
Have no fear when you stare in the mirror,
Never let small minds make you feel inferior,
Every scar, every mark is a snippet of our story,
So remember,
Confidence is key don't ever feel guilty about it,
You're not responsible for what they see so let them be
   threatened by it.

Identity

WORDS BY <u>Hiba</u>

As soon as I enter the room...
My identity speaks for me.
My struggles.
My experiences...
But most of all my story.

You see for centuries my coloniser
had tried to handcuff me
away from ever
finding anything about my
identity. My history.
Stolen history.

I mean I watched my own mother tongue fall into the arms of
   its coloniser.
I'm more familiar with his language than I am of my own.
I'm more accustomed to his western life... than I am of my own.
And I know I am not alone when I say this.

I have questions.
Questions which are kept quietly tucked into the side.
Like who are my heroes?
My ancestors?
Tell me about their struggles.
Their triumphs.
Their trails.
Tell me more about the soil...
The soil that make up my grounds.
My roots.

Yet all these questions are left unanswered.
But I guess it's standard.
I mean after all
what did I expect?
Answers!

Wish I could have been with the hujjaj

WORDS BY Samira

They be trying it on.
I'm just trying to stay calm.
Fasting like it's Ramadan.
Trying to increase my iman and stay away from haram.
It's a time for sacrifice and giving alms.
Wish I could have been with the Hujjaj up in masjid al haram;
     but it's calm.
InshaaAllah my time will come for me to do the pilgrimage.
Need to tick it off the bucket list,
like I did with the pyramids.
Yeah, I like to live a bit.
Islam's my way of life so I try living it.
It's a time for sacrifice so I'm giving it away if I'm not needing it.
Even if I'm wanting it.
Jannah is the goal and I'm hunting it.

Magic in our melanin

WORDS BY Georgia

We have magic in our melanin,
But we have forgotten how to fly,
And to the young black men in London,
I want to know why!
Why mothers are crying for the loss of their sons,
Grieving, for their boys, so young.
And it's not like this has just begun,
It's been going on for years,
The London streets hold the memories of every mother's tears.
Letting their son go out at night has become a mother's biggest fear.
Damn.
We have magic in our melanin,
And we need to fly.

Nichola

WORDS BY Acafella

I commute to King's Cross station every morning and as I emerge
from the underground the forgotten almost immediately appear.
I think about how horrible it would be to feel stranded and lonely
with thousands of people near...

I spotted a woman with tears streaming down her face
and hundreds of people walking past without so much as tilting
their heads. They could have shared some kind words, *"you don't
exist"* is what they unintentionally said.

Her name was Nichola, I didn't hear much of her story but I heard
enough to make me sad. Just 15 minutes before I was scorned for
listening to music loudly by the same person who strolled passed
Nichola like she didn't exist - interesting, the different kind of
things that make people mad...

It's distressing to see our fellow human beings in trouble,
if we tackled these problems as one I think they'd be fixed on
the double!

For those feeling hopeless and living lives of despair, is a minimum
of dialogue not something we could all share?

I can't tell you how many times I've tried to promote compassion
to be countered with a story of a single moment where an offering
of food was rejected. You'd think homelessness was a disease and
showing kindness is how you get infected.

When and where we can - we should try to practice kindness,
especially in weathers where temperatures are measured in the
minus...

Some don't even shake their heads or spare a thought for those
without beds. No love for those wearing incomplete clothing
or addicts dressed in items with loose threads, for me it's like
watching people drown in water on the spot while I tread. Spikes
on the floor for those rarely fed, you didn't just walk past, up you
sped, *"probably spend it on booze or drugs"* that's what you said. If

this sounds like you, I'm not automatically suggesting you're a bad person, just clearly easily lead.

Imagine if villages really did raise children, my village has a population of around 8 million. That's a lot of voices, a lot of power, picture the smiles instead of the usual glower. Imagine them screaming in support + belief, as we cultivate success and provided relief.

What a beautiful thought and spectacular sight, looking out for one another, helping in times of plight...

Let's start with communication, after all we are only separated by less than 6 degrees of separation.

Using dialogue as a civic duty, our tongues will acknowledge the pain detected from our eyes' scrutiny.

There should be no 'others' just sisters and brothers. If you don't care have some words with yourself. Complicity and silence sentences people like Nichola to hell...

The District Line busker

WORDS BY Danny

"Dear ladies and gentlemen,

Sorry to bother you on your work commute. I understand you wanna be left alone and you're probably just heading home. I want you to know that I pray to be you...

I'm currently looking for you to be kind, even a cigarette'll do

A pound would be appreciated, I'm just trying to get some food.

Oh you have no spare change, Mr Armani Suit

Well either way I offer you a blessed day because I have no malice in my heart for you"

Even when you looked down when I attempt eye contact.
Even when you scuttled your shoes backwards in case I dare brush past your feet with mine.
Even when you disregarded my plight as if I am not quite, a human.

I busk upon the district line with my paper cup as my drum, I beat its skin with my pain and loose change sounds as my cymbal.

I've been performing the same song for longer than I want to remember, wheel it out like a Frank Sinatra ballad at a karaoke bar.

Each rendition packs less soul than the last. Like a band who knows the glory days are behind them. The paper cup just doesn't drum the same. The pain louder than the cymbal.

I wonder how many people won't look at me today.

Still the busker must busk.

"Dear ladies and gentlemen

Sorry to bot...

We Are Nation

WORDS BY Marlon

From an adopted corner of London I think of home.
And slowly hum the national anthem
As my forgotten island writhes beneath the waters
Of her nature's latest tantrum.
The news that filtered through to me that day,
Was of the roof tops of rum shops
That had finally come to rest
In the estuary where we used to catch our tri' tri' fish.

So I held my breath......

As if it were I was being swept beneath the barely standing bridges,
A coconut husk of a man whisked away
Among the palms and flotsam,
Turning over and over like a-half-a-slippers.

They said the roads became rivers,
And the rivers became aggression.
Throbbing veins of topsoil,
An Exodus of life and all possession.

And As the death toll rose to ten there was still nothing on the BBC,
But a cluster of scientists got themselves stuck in some Antarctic ice,
No room in the headlines for we.

So my fellow mercenary wonderers and I gathered,
Remotely,
Subdued but glued to our devices.
Awaiting stories of survival,
Told by distant voices from the crisis.

From an adopted corner of London I think of home,
And slowly hum...

I loved you like myself

WORDS BY <u>Mequannt</u>

ልክ እንደራሴ አወድሻ ነበረ
ልክ እንደራሴ አወድሻ ነበረ
ልጠይቅ ባስበው ህሊናየ አፈረ
ጊዜየን ጨረስኩት ሳይሽ በማፈር
አንድ ቀን አይቼሽ ገባሽ ወይ ከልቤ
ማነው የገረሽ በፍቅር መራቤ
መናገር አልችልም ፊት ለፊት ቀርቤ
ፍቅሬን ልግለፅልሽ ፀፊ በደብዳቤ
መመላለሻየ የፍቅር ወደቤ
እንችን ካየሁ ወዱህ ተረበሽ ልቤ
ፍቅር ይዞው ነበር ምድቤ ምድብቤ
እንድም ላላፈቅር ላልፀናፍም ደብዳቤ
ላምን ትገቢያለሽ ከተዘጋው ልቤ
መግባቱንስ ግቢው አይከፋው ሆዴ
ግን አይቼሽ ከቀረሁ አይቀር መናደዴ
እኔስ ተጓኙ ነበርኩ የፍቅር ነጋዴ
መልስ ያጣ ሁላት አየከፈው ሆዴ
በመልክም ብነግድ ትርፍ እንደልብ ነው
የሚያግደኝ የለም ውጪኛው አካል ነው
በዝ ናም ብነግድ ትርፍ አቅም በላይ ነው
በጊዜው ብነግድ እነር የሚያቀው ነው
እኔን ያከሰረኝ በልብሽ ስነግድ
በፍቅርሽ ያስገባኝ ፀባይሽ ብቻ ነው
ፍቅርሽ ከብዶብኛል ታዲያ እንዴት ልቻለው
ህሳቤን ተረጀው እንድንካፈለው
መጠየቅ ባይከብድም መፍራት አይቀሬ ነው
እኔን የጎዳኝ መቀራሬቤ ነው፡፡
እስኪ ሰላም ብየ ልግለፅልሽ ፍቅሬ
መቾም አያስቀይም የሆዴን መንገሬ
ካየሁሽ እስካሁን አለሁ ተቸግሬ
ያን ወጎ ፍቅር ከጀርባየ አዝየ
በቃላት ቅንብር ጠራሁ የኔ ብየ
እንዳችም መልስ ስጭኝ ወይ በይኝ ፍቅርየ
እንዲህ ስፀፍልሽ እኔ ተቸግሬ
እንካን ቅር እንዲልሽ ብነ አይደለም ፍቅሬ
እራሴን ለመመምራት በጣም ተቸግሬ
እንዴት ይሻለኛል ንገሪኝ ፍቅርየ

ልክ እንደራሴ አወደሽ ነበረ
ማፍቀር ግን ከባድ ነው ቅድም እያሰበረ
እንዲህ ስፀፍልሽ እንዳይልሽ ቅር
ምንም አዲስ አይደል በጊዜ ማፍቀር
ፍቅሬን ብገልፀልሽ በስጋት ቁጠር
አይን የያመጣው እዳ ከዚያው ተወርውሮ
በፍፁም አይቀርም ፍቅር ተሰውሮ
ጎንድ እጅ ወርውሮ ሁለት ወፍ መግደል
የተለመደ ነው በኛቤት በሀል
እንዲህ ሳንጋራኑር በቃላት እምቄ
የኔን ማፍቀር እንጅ ያንችን የት እውቄ
ብዙ ይገጥመዋል ሰው ሲፍር በሂወት
እንዲህም በሁለቶች መደሰት መከፋት
አድር ግሽ አትይው ማፍቀር እንደ ጥፋት

Fear of Separation

WORDS BY Ahmed

When I glimpse the moon
It reminds me of your beauty
Your loyalty as a mistress
Then it flies me into - the entire universe
Stars, Milky Way
With immense, wild imaginations
It heats the lust of love within me
And turns me to a blind lover
As the past says, *"love is blind"*
I confess that's true
I can't see myself
While I'm deprived
From your enchanting love
I beg you, don't burn me
In the twinkling of fire
With your separation
Let me be in your arms
Brimming with peace and love

Every Time You're High

WORDS BY Billy

now I realize

Every time you're high
I'm always forgotten in your bloodshot eyes

Edges & World

WORDS BY Sophie

Edges

With you,
I breathe into my edges.
It's deep blue,
And bone white.

World

When a person becomes a world
You're pulled sideways, dragged
Your body,
into some other orbit.
It takes you by surprise, their gravity,
The intensity
The strength of love's force
Pulling you across their Skies.
Like the moon across the night,
Horizon to Horizon,
across their skin like Clouds.
You're drawn into their centre.
Dive beneath their surface,
Swim into their deep.

House at the End of the World

WORDS BY Travis

There is a house
On the edge of it all
Swirling wall of flame between the dark and the light

There is a woman
And there is a man
Every night they complete the pact to keep the dark from the light

There is a game
As old as time
The players play, make the moves set in stone, the oldest game

There are creatures
That live in the dark
If the game is not played they journey into the light

The creatures they wear
Faces of your friends
Eyes, ear, mouths, nose, you don't know they are coming until it far
    too late

The woman moves
The man counters
On and on it goes into the night, each turn of the earth the game
    is played

The game last
For many turns
Until the man's throat is slit and the pact is done

The woman cries
Tears of sorrow
The man she loved she kills again

Each day they wake
Renewed once more
The keep the pact they swore in stone, to protect me and to
    protect you from the creatures that live in the dark

The woman cries
And the man knows not
Of the sacrifice she makes each night

Old they are
Older than all
They remember the world before time was born

Hungry they are
Hungrier than all
If the woman falter just once they slip into the light

Chase me to the end of the world
Where there lives a sheet of flame
Higher than the heavens it burns
To the house at the end of the world

CUNTO

WORDS BY <u>Joelle</u>

(i) The Body as a Battleground

some girls fall from sunlight skies/ straight down into flat-pack
floral dresses/ grab their smiles from a hook behind the door/
rescue their faces/ from rip tides of mirrors//
some girls are always

falling.

you fall/ miss your body entirely/ land somewhere in enemy
territory/ behind the lines/ body a foreign country/ you cannot get
a visa for/ skin a parachute caught in tree branches// you awaken in
no man's land/ gunfire from over the horizon/ women/ crucified on
hashtags across the dark hills.

your trench is crowded with dead women/ wearing faces that try
to escape them/ & the clothes of someone you once knew// there
are landmines buried deep beneath your skin/ no one understands
them/ *tread carefully when you walk across me*// in between the
battle cry and the bedroom/ is this sticky quiet/ this no man's land/
& this/ is where you live.

men explode when you least expect it.

you will spend your life searching for your body.

(iv) The Body as Political Placard

You don't wear make-up/ to prove/ you have not made anything
up/ this is your face/ your father's friends gave it to you/ one
Christmas eve in 1973/ you unwrapped it beneath a decorated
tree/ from which the rest of your family hung. They sip cocktails
as you disappear, swaying gently to the wail of celebration, that
harbinger of party.

You cut your first suit out of the thick silence when you enter
a room.

(vii) The Body as A Haunted House

In sleep/ my body is a haunted house/ there are footsteps along
fallopian corridors/ the corridor is a rope strung above a mouth/
I am woken by blurred voices without bodies/ quiet arguments/
in the basement// once I was possessed/ by a small girl/ who
looked the same as me/ who self-immolated on a Sunday
afternoon/ whose parents were downstairs/ hardwiring
hangovers/ whose Christmas songs/ played in nooses/ my heart
is a church bell/ but nobody visits/ & God is a man/ with his hands
in his pockets/ watching.

Ear

WORDS BY <u>Leanne</u>

I might superglue my head to your chest

On the side of my right ear
It'll be nuzzled (and when I say nuzzled, I mean superglued)
   to your hairy, hairy chest

I'll tune into the sound of your unassuming heartbeat
All muffled and dull like someone's having a party two doors down

The left ear will remain, perfectly at one with the ether
Very suitable for hearing other things

Such as:
- A microwave ping
- A washing machine whirl
- A WhatsApp message coming through
- The theme tune to the news
- Someone tapping on a computer keyboard
- Someone tapping on the window
- Someone tap-dancing

My vision will be impaired, for sure
My head at an acute angle
Looking down at the floor like I'm sad
But I'm not
I'm just
I'm just
I'm just Chasing Pavements
Even if it leads no where
. . . yeah

(The tapping at the window's still going)

It's quite a purposeful banging now
The smash is loud, despite only hearing it in mono

I go to look up but can't on accounts of my head being superglued
   to your chest

I push my finger deep into the exposed ear
And squeeze shut my downtrodden eyes

I feel a bit of cold dribble down my fused bonce
My head is grabbed and yanked and lifted with great impetus like
    it's the World Cup

We are, quite literally, torn apart

I look down
Bits of my hair are stuck to your chest
And bits of *your* hair are stuck to my face

I look up
And she's there
Holding a massive cotton bud like she's a contestant on Gladiators
It drips with white spirit

She looks at my weary eyes and bold patches
I start to pick the bits of chest hair from my skull
And she stops me
And she says, *"It is alright, isn't it"*
And it is.

October

WORDS BY Wendy

Thank you,
For the mistake made,
My gain,
Broken through the pain.

My finding,
I'm breathing,
No more rehearsal,
I'm alive.

Getting it right,
I'm discovered again.

Unleash eternity within me

WORDS BY Natasha

Let's sip coffee and share our secrets.

Tell me your late-night feelings. The ones that leave you tangled
and hot underneath your sheets. The ones where your breathe
would get heavy against my neck, as the fantasy becomes the
sweet reality.

Lay with me after when we are left open, Pandora's box unleashed
and your arms around me.

Let's make eternity in our love. Let it be written amongst the stars.
For there is no one like us.

To the Birds

WORDS BY Mr Gee

.

Two Red Robins awoke early one morning,
Father & Son sharing a moment of calling,
In the magical hours between dew drops & dawn,
When all is calm with the world,

.

Said Son to Father: *"Dad why do we sing?"*
And puff up our chests & limber up our wings,
It seems to me, to be a bird is but a lowly thing,
When man is in charge of this world,

.

He builds a nest so high, that it can make love to the sky,
He wears feathers in all colours, in all shapes & sizes,
His wings are invisible, yet he flies so high,
So why should we sing in this world?

.

Said the Father to the Son: *"Yes Man indeed is strong"*
He's proud as a peacock & has the grace of a swan,
He even goes a little cuckoo, when the weather goes wrong,
For he believes he's in charge of this world,

.

He puts a feather in his cap & tries to rule the roost,
But whenever he gets scared he feels the bump of a goose,
Because we used to be dinosaurs & that's the truth,
And my Son, that's why we'll always sing in this world.

.

Invisible Man

WORDS BY <u>basq-Lyon</u>

Part I

I am invisible.
You can't see me cos you don't want to.
It's fine,
cos while you stay blind I will rise.

I am invisible.
I live, lost, between your misconceptions and agendas.

See,
black could never be separated from the boy,
and nothing changes when you're a teen,
and it seems to stick even stronger to the man.

So I was a black boy,
Then a black teen,
Now a black man,
Yet I still seek,
For an identity outside of that.

It's only since I began accepting my invisibility,
that I do not bother seeking out my oppressor to take responsibility,
now that I have the authority,
to shape my own destiny.

I wasted my energy trying to,
convince your ignorance,
battling through micro-aggressions,
whilst facing adolescence.

I wasted my energy trying to,
fight feelings of frustration,
when failing,
to change your false perceptions.

So now I'm claiming back my sentence,
and replacing it with silence.

Because right now:
finding my voice,
is more important than making noise.

I am invisible.
You can't see me cos you don't want to.
It's fine,
cos while you stay blind I will rise.

Part II

When I look into a black man's eyes I see pride.
The ability to hold it together,
while fighting to survive,
against the odds set for others to thrive.

When I look into the a black man's mannerisms,
I see there: hidden,
a special tradition.
When a brother of similar skin tone crosses,
our path we exchange a nod or slight upward jolt of the chin,
and although words can't quite pinpoint its significance,
that nod is rooted in black excellence.

When I look into a black man's skin,
I see how tense the rest of his body is,
and how the muscles strain under the weight his carrying.

Yet it's proven that,
Like his skin he don't crack-
So he let's weight rest on his back-
Even though he knows that means he may never relax.

But you don't see that, do you?
You misinterpret the fire in his eyes,
for desire to antagonise,
as you project generalised ideas of black identity,
you fail to see his humanity.

You only see the surface of our mannerisms,
adopt the ones that suit you,
ignoring their significance,

only acknowledging the culture when convenient,
neglecting the foundations that it's rooted it in.

You see an athlete,
a rapper 'saved' from the streets,
and think it represents our whole community.

You see our body for profit,
only valued when we rap or kick something.

Fetishized for the size of our...
Redefined and described with restrictive characteristics.

You see skin deep.
I see fire.

You see Stormzy.
I see Merky's empire.
You see black hands.
I see a future that's brighter.

You see the stereotype, and I see the outliers.

You see an outburst,
But not micro-aggressions that came first.

You see,
this selective vision,
gives you a false impression,
cos what you see,
and what I see when I look in the mirror,
are very different.

But while you remain blind,
I'll watch my people rise,
and build our own empire,
break boundaries and inspire.

I am invisible.
You can't see me cos you don't want to.
It's fine, cos while you stay blind we will rise.

"*High visibility renders one invisible*" Ralph Ellison.

Untitled

WORDS BY <u>Joel</u>

Well I found it when I let go
Headed home inside my headphones
I tried to live the way they told me
I couldn't stay inside the red cones

I took a breath and then I leaned back
Then they took away the bean bags
I've got so used to living broken
Didn't notice that my screen cracked

Tired eyes trying to earn all your love
Alcohol only stings the dirt in my cuts
I try and hide behind the hurt in my guts
Holding out a thumb to the cars
Yet here we are

I was hoping for so much more
Boxing a bear with a broken jaw
I only knew when I hit the floor
Somebody loves me after all

Change

WORDS BY <u>Sade</u>

Battered by a change in the wind
Sudden and unexpected
Full force
With magnitude and attitude

Just the clothes
On our tender backs
Confused and subdued
Without water and food

Where to run
Where to hide
What will happen
To me and my child
Terrified

When we talked truth
They were not shocked
When we sought help
They jeered and they mocked

Shelter
Suddenly an important status to have
Who and what
Would hide us
Providing security and not wrath

Learning to defend ourselves
Trying to be brave
Having to pretend
That this is not the end

Wounded, tired, lonely
Scared and oppressed
Persecuted, downtrodden
And bereft

Hostility, aggression
Confrontation and hate
An arduous
Unpredictable encounter

That made us desolate
A future
A hope
Dreamt of and prayed for
Flowing abundantly
Agape love

Judgement

WORDS BY <u>Ezra</u>

Battling with my Demons while trying to win a war against society
Both battles I'm trying to win against so I can finally be at peace
with my sanity
I feel weakened by the judgement I constantly face in my life
Most of the time opinions were made before I've even given them
anything to judge
It's like my whole entire persona was being smeared, into
the nothingness...
Is this all I am? Am I just a nuisance? Was I ever a somebody?
Their perspective plagued my mind causing paranoia of ones
own identity
But also, paranoia of all the existing things of this world I live in
So I say my prayers at night, is the world eavesdropping,
listening in?
Trying to rebel against my greatness, so I can remain
uncomfortable in my own skin
I know my life has more meaning so I yearn to travel the world to
see what else life has for me
But poverty has built this imprisonment to make me feel like, this is
the only home for me
Not allowing me to think or see outside the box.

But then I realised if society is trying to hold me down so
much, that means I have a powerful gift to uplift, maybe even
a generation
Solving meaningful complication
And resisting against their manipulation
I need to strive towards my calling, so I can at last find my answers
So I made up mind, I needed to totally set myself free of
their judgment
Because I felt so clouded by their opinions dismissed from seeing
the clear blue sky
But still without a clear view above I have drawn a masterpiece in
my mind
As above so below
The system I will overthrow
So my consciousness will prevail
Look in my eyes the windows to my soul

Lives the supreme intelligence of my inner world that even this
outer world couldn't comprehend
So there's no need to wander outer space if I've already found my
inner peace
Never again, I couldn't let myself play into their distraction
Feeding their satisfaction
If I did, that'll be me falling into their deepest delusions and
fragile fantasy's
Leaving me with no reality.

What do you give a man that has nothing? You give him a reason.
A purpose to live
So I purposely give you this side of me
To let my art live through me to create, build and execute all angles
of creation so I can inspire the collective consciousness all over
the nations
Some of us shine in the sunlight, others glow in the darkness, .
it's just the timing of the universe
My destiny is destined I have faith in my fate
I may have suffered along the way
But every tear drop was the substance needed to the rising seed
of my success.
Inner peace is what I strive for, nothing less.

AAVEnues

WORDS BY <u>Legacy</u>

i know anita hill must have had her fair share of olivia pope nights _
     those evenings locked away with nothing between her and
the world but a functioning peephole and a glass of merlot !

that place of peace that comes with being steps away from a
clawfoot tub
(1) in an apartment that you own outright (2) if those tax breaks let
you live right the hiss of
        television suicidal / that tub-teeter playing tug-of-war
        with a toothy
     plug gumming at a gaping socket {{gotta love that booty}}

olivia pope and annalise keating have that in common tho
~
     that particular brand of *post-black* that means you can
take a [straight/white/male] life in the name of justice
     and it somehow shakes out to a fair trade [it's NBD]

#girlbye : that liberty makes me jealous af

i'm thirsty for such a high-functioning fiction ~~~ smh i envy a
good assassination followed by a bottle of vodka to block out the
audacity of this america
     [isn't that just the definition of imagination]

doesn't "amerigo vespucci" sound like your designer handbag?
     do you follow him on twitter?

who knew the legacy of pangea would be
     overwritten via the supremacy of autocorrect
     !!!!!

this street view was from, like, centuries ago don't believe the
route on google maps:

bb when we were all connected

everything was in walking distance and
              those bipedal motherfuckers got their steps in ALL DAY

~~~~this is the dream! yes, we can have it! yes, we can do it!~~~~

this utopic trajectory toeing the edge of anthropocene // _
anthropocene_ is my ***fav***

ahahaha
!
what can we rebrand the name of this weird instant when
considering advancing eco-conditions as a mode of mass genocide
          // is an industrial complex, like, an actual complex? Kk.

those precious moments always lie perfectly across my tongue like a
good tab of acid

why can't we just ghost on russia they're fugly with their nerve
agents: *sigh*

life is just so newsy these days

          i'm so O V E R facebook as a governmental body
          i'm all about the one who played the lawyer on sex in the city
          for governor
                    what's a working families party - - - sounds super fun?!?

doesn't it feel like daily there is a new
t$unami
          ~when the time comes FEMA will be doing *dinner and a
movie* with its boo and will send us all to voicemail [sorry, can't talk
right now]

at this point i'm getting mixed up about which direction the water is
coming from
          but what i know for real is that we are all going under so i
          better find my floaties

if you don't know what i'm talking about this isn't for you!!!!!

when we put our palms in the air and pledge to tell the *whole
truth* and ****nothing but the truth**** we know that god will sit
up straight and pay attention

woke right alongside the rest of the
nation
{{amerigo too}}

can't we leave these cute lil colombus-wannabes alone!!!!!
all they wanna do is blast quavo in their digital blackface //
a proliferation of

memes screaming
YAS

those forefathers weren't my
daddy

you steal from us every day //

don't think that I missed you pocketing that VineTM affect,

i'm dead i'm not
dumb

this femme business is complicated
tho

no, like, literally it is a business get the memo:
the proof is in Post Malone's beauty channel that
YouTube vibe showing us how to flat iron our bangs

black is beautiful!!!!!! TM
this fractal feminist futurity is super wack!!!!!!

bill cosby once our national daddy is going to jail –
!
but clarence thomas gets to high-five brett kavanaugh on his
way to the supreme court? Kk. call this meta.

i wonder if brett will dance like theresa may in secret now that he's
out of detention

who will make that phone call, to teach him how to move his
virgin hips

i didn't know virgins were incapable of violence _ thanx for the DM _
!
so glad someone is praying with their little girls tonight that's so
new-wave
        [but – wait – did the immaculate conception ask for consent?]

i'm feeling some kinda way!

especially because my own father even agreed before he died - - -
that this cosby thing might be some kind of bigger conspiracy

this is what world-making looks like :::: that part of the patriarchy
that eats itself like a baloney sandwich from blimpie
        & then netflix and chills &
        ghosts on tinder hopefuls

IDK ~ when o'hara had that queer coke was he grateful to at least
be seated?!?!?
        i know it was probs super yummy and maybe this is petty but
isn't it kinda problematic is that my aunt had to go home to drink
from her own sink?

        ^ is blackness stickier than cola? is it sweeter? ^

see, this is the problem with politics these days : everyone is out for
themselves
all these trees keep dying because they keep getting skin-stripped
for switches
        those injurious tongues waiting to be activated
        line-items in the expense report of
        capitalism

here's a meme: those viral videos of us running !

that thing that is commonplace on my finsta feed !
        but when we see it in childish gambino's new vid ! suddenly
        there's proof ~~ it's ! really ! real !

are quaaludes OR one beer part of the racial imaginary? {pick one.}

when you meme these memorable instants are your gifs paying
homage to the faith we kept while in middle passage which tbh
probs inspired the invention of remix itself?

*** i have questions tho ****

i know it isn't en vogue right now but all this makes me want to die

the other night i felt inspired by that drone lyfe
      so followed a girl home off the utica stop on the A train
      {{i just wanted to hear her position on jeff flake}}

           girl I see you // can you be my witness
           too?!?

FWIW her boyfriend ***just didn't get it***
      {went on and on about that new eckhaus latta show at the
      whitney tho}

what stands between us and the world ~ ?
      is it a peephole, can i get another glass of wine to forget
      this feeling pls

those flashes to nights where :

           →→→→ had my hair pulled without permission and
           →→→→→→→ where i ran barefoot because the other option
           was to never run again

the best ragers are bipartisan babe ::::: i'm a bipartisan
bae

what really happened in that elevator my third eye started
bleeding // did i miss it?!?!?!?!

was that feminism!!!!!
      {{wait - is jeff an ally? ugh can we LOVE HIM}}

did flake feel similar feels to when solange had her justice on jay-z

      NO ONE CHEATS ON BEY!!!! →→→→ without later turning
the mess of marriage into millions :
           it's payback @ its best
           remember all these
           struggles
                  can be yours
                  too

who will be in Bey's corner today // and can us bbz be bey 2day 2?!?
save us!!!!!!

    when yoko said ****woman is the nigger of the world****
did she think of zora neale [[who flagged that moon first - - - ?]]

those sliding doors were held just in time~~~~!

    the eyes of all cameras blinking curiously under the sun of
    sudden celebrity
        that tan is counterrevolutionary ::::: apolitical but chic af

i don't care if you don't think i deserve a living wage
    the bernie bros say we can have one SO THERE!!!!!!!

i am one stumble away from having to pay full rent for air and water
    let me tell you it isn't cleaner up here

i feel super bummed about those women who keep trying to get
a seat at the table but stay hungry this is chess // just keep playing
~~~~ you aren't here to eat

babe that dress is super cute YAS!
    yes it matches his dockers true
    but
        wait i don't think he gives a fuck about you tho
        {{remember that}}

voter suppression isn't pussy power ::::: put your hat away

    are you going to the rally
    2nite?

        get me the t-shirt that says "let america be america
        again"
            i'm voting for langston // he was right all along
            about you—

MOONSONG

WORDS BY <u>Azareen</u>

i dreamt i was drowning in a swell
waters rising
no higher place in sight
grandmother, aunt, uncle: all dead
having expended their capitol of grief early
i felt you breathing next to me
you whom i love
from the space of my childhood
like i have never loved anybody
i instruct myself to get out of the darkness
the humid waters that reek of
corpses shot
standing shoulder-to-shoulder
my life sown to the borders of their death
make no mistake
you who suffer my deaths
the body-count
even though you do not know it
the swell of the waters is
as much mine as it is yours
it only appears as though i am here alone
drowning in the waters of the dead
my dead
who are not yours
though you will have your own
in the morning i walk down the avenue
wind shearing my face
aware that i am writing
a poem unworthy of the dead
who hang from its words
how do i tell you
that i am the child of mortal enemies
this land into which i was born
& that land on which i was raised
the dead faceless in the rusty glow of the moon
i made garlands of the weeping willows
magnolia of childhood
from where i love you

where i made believe
unaware that the life i was living
would become a ghost
old the briberies
the contracts signed
the corrupt dealings
the bodies eliminated
the give me this & i will let you
have thats
but
imagine i return to tell you
cheeks flushed from the cold
imagine a whole life
become ethereal
imagine
staring
at
your
own
ghost

The Shores Of Calais

WORDS BY <u>Joanna</u>

A thousand miles they have walked,
Forced to flee their homes,
Bombs tore apart the night sky,
And terror filled their bones.

Sat askew a dinghy boat,
Their souls clinging on for life,
The choppy waters do their worst,
And a passenger lost his wife.

The voyage must continue on,
Smacked by a violent wave,
They drown out the husbands cries,
Gone forever, deep into her grave.

Finally, ashore, the boat does reach,
Not a moment for her mourning,
A sombre barefoot march begins,
Soon forgotten was her drowning.

Towards a land that is free and just,
Liberty from lynching and war,
Soon they will reach their safe haven,
But peace in their heart will be nevermore,

Upon the sludge ridden shores of Calais,
Rubber bullets and teargas to subdue,
The savagery of slum life,
Peace won't be found here, they knew.

A thousand miles they have walked,
We hear their freedom call,
Stuck in the horrors of purgatory,
For this isn't freedom at all !

Untitled

WORDS BY Briona

To travel 3,000 miles from a place called home
Just to realize that home ain't what it's supposed to be
But what a sad dichotomy
To be halfway across the world
And still not know who you are

It's an empty feeling to constantly yearn for a place you've
    never been
But that lives within you

It's in the reach of my arms
The span of my hips
The stride of my step
The curl of my lips *(Maya Angelou)*

To be a representative of a place that treats you as disposable
But that continues to save you over again
America ain't shit without black people
But I don't know who I am without America

People always ask me where I'm from
And I'm trying to make peace with the silence and shoulder shrugs
    to come
As I find pieces of myself in every corner of the world.

Culture Clash

WORDS BY Vanessa

who you are
has been covered up
for so long.
you bend & break

and
    t
      w
    i
     s
    t
and

shape
to find your place
in society's mould.

but
truth be told
this life, that you live, is a lie
the real you
is hidden inside.
a spiritual sensitive soul
arising from the birthplace of gold.
this eclectic mix
of your heritage,
two tribes
intertwined,
Ghanaian - British.

a light source beams
from your innermost being
illuminating
the dark-ridden sky,
a stride in your step
as you dare not forget,
you must walk
with your ancestors' pride.

an elegant collective
of powerful women,
submitted to the Lord,
the Most High.

rest assured
that you're on the right path,
unlearning
social constructs
which kept you bound
from discovering
who you truly are.
your existence
requires
a commitment,
to connect
with your truest self.
a raw awakening
once you partake in
this quest,
where you'll surely
prevail.

Petaled hope

WORDS BY Luke

the women marched for us;
joined arms carrying
sleeping flowers in hand,
through August's baking Balkan
sun,
casting jubilant shadows upon pavements won
the women marched for me;
with accomplished smiles and hearts aligned –
under the Skopje clouds of war
their voices a symphony of bees in tempest
swarming
the Balkan women marched for
themselves;
that day and in that way,
as our toe caps ring-fenced their fervent
strides, our holstered iron
was no match
for the liberated hearts
petaled by a hope in womankind.

So, where are you from?

WORDS BY Ruby

Too foreign for here,

Too foreign for there,

Too foreign for anywhere.

Sleeper Train

WORDS BY Sharmay

I met a girl from Kazakhstan on the sleeper train from Luxor
   to Cairo.
For ten hours we shared a cabin.
Although our mouths did not make the same shapes and sounds,
Our eyes shared a mutual excitement for feluccas,
And our smiles told us we felt the same way about the Nile.
When the comprehension was thin,
Our exaggerated shrugs were visual signs that we were giving up
   on our differences,
And we chose to bridge the gap with laughter,
Something our spirits could understand.
And so we laughed at all things that connected us:
The oppressive heat that melted our foreheads,
The rhythmic creaking of our carriage that favoured a
   whinnying horse,
The games of noughts and crosses we played in her notebook,
The animal silhouettes we made with our hands as the light faded.
In Cairo we disembarked with an eagerness to continue
   our journeys,
And a twinge of sadness for the goodbye.
Two strangers,
Finding that the world is small
And the people in it are far more alike than they are different.

Not my country, my place

WORDS BY Aarushi

I made my fortune at the slots
I wore new perfume at dinner
I read words that I could almost feel
I ate a full pizza in one sitting
I lay in the ocean with my son
I painted strokes straight from my gut
I thought about blue and green in the afternoon
I smiled my happiest smile at her
I hid from the rain for two hours
I hugged a penguin

I tried to find home today
I ran fast and hid well today
I thought about the lost heirloom today
I felt safe as I took a walk today
I missed my mother's cooking today
I learned new things at school today
I didn't feel afraid today
I found a new world to belong to today

Untitled

WORDS BY Katy

A home is not just a house,
Covered in bricks and cement,
A home is where you feel safe and content,
Or surrounded by whom or what you love.

Volta

WORDS BY Fran

way back, when we didn't know better, fidgety
as poltergeists in the paralysed logic of classrooms.
they call us *cusses*. we scallied the asphalt, kicking
at weeds. kids in clusters. empty bellies spread in
umbels out of the power-cut-dark of sites, estates;
of tenancies and tenements, of anywhere a staircase
stinks of piss. way back. a pigeon-chested crewcut,
growing wizened as a monkey's paw; bent by asthma,
lack of sun. girls, with the furtive looks of prison
snitches. big brothers sniffing, in the ordinance of their
acne. sisters, faces terraformed by tubes of shoplifted
revlon. but we was free. or felt as if. us names were
not infinite misprint, didn't look into the mirror then,
and know usselves for hoax. not *english-english*, see?
not how it counts. this englishness is thoroughbred,
exemplary and fatal; talks in jargons of duress.
its symphony makes skeletons. way back we hadn't
learnt their petty quintessentials, or applied them to
usselves. but one by one we fell. to skite or spleen.
to politics or heroin, its mute omertà meant to
immunise against this hurt. we saw ourselves for
dirty and we took their names to heart. way back,
when we knew better, how we'd strut and thrust
though the english real. no exile, that great virus,
squirming in our partial blood. back before
the factions and the flags; a million divisions
along chromosomes and postcodes. when we were
kids, just kids, that mad insomniac splinter group,
starry conquerors of sleep.

I am not a witch

WORDS BY <u>Simon</u>

You only deliver justice with a timer switch
promising *my turn will come.*

I am not a witch.

I am still targeted or beaten up
for ramming fear down your throat,
spite sticks in your teeth, then spews on my feet.
Even that will not scratch such infernal itch,
wiping me off your world's face.

I am not a witch.

Tied hands, feet, to metronomic ducking stools,
all those other tools of naked oppression.
Evading your hag hunts, escaping round-up camps
where I'd end up digging, ending in a ditch.
I won't bury your shame.

I am not a witch.

Expelled or locked up
in cell of stale air, with coal-tarred lungs, I gasp.
Choked by vitriol dripping from drenched fists.
Foretasting your final punch, my lips tremble, then twitch;
huddled, shuddering, I cry,

I am not a witch!

Though when it suits you, we're eagerly paraded
as those with veiled powers and special features:
clowned-up cheap old fools making you laugh.
Guess that's straight privilege for the entitled rich:
using my bent ass as you wish.

I am not a witch.

Lauded for cross-gartered tragic comedy acts,
self-damnation goes where you've been all along.
But dark humour laughs in echoes around you:
seduced by tickles, twinkles or a camp bitch,
you fall for gravity tricks.

I am not a witch.

To survive your world I need hidden powers,
overcoming self-hate with spells, incantations,
rituals of shamans, faeries, seers and diviners.
Swallowing soul medicine to heal and enrich.
Perhaps, after all, maybe

I am but a witch.

My stop

WORDS BY Conor

The driver noticed an old gas station drawing closer as the truck rolled down the highway. He saw a lone figure standing by the disused gas pumps. Unlike most hitchers the silhouette did not have a hopeful thumb stuck out into the road. Instead the woman - for now he could see it was a woman - simply stood, two hands holding a large carrier bag by her feet. The driver stopped. The woman knocked on the passenger door and at the drivers signal, opened it and lay her bag in the space between the seats. After a swift exchange of greetings, the truck rumbled into first and pulled away.

It had been some three quiet hours since the passenger had got on. The surrounding expanse of desert was empty, save for occasional brush. The earth was flat and cracked.
Without warning the passenger said, *"What do you carry?"* She gestured toward the hold. *"In the back."*
"You're not from round here, are you?" The driver asked.
"Is anyone?" She replied.
They both smiled and he began listing the items that were stored in the hold.
"Bedside tables... bedside lamps... tables, beds, lamps..."
The woman was silent.
The driver's discomfort had subsided and he began to talk in his miscellaneous drawl. *"You know this man asked me for change the other day, first thing he said was 'I'm sorry'. I mean, 'I'm sorry'? sorry for what? Five seconds after I passed him I had to go back and give him everything I had. You know he said? 'I'm sorry.' Poor guy, that really got to me."*
The woman nodded and replied, *"Maybe... he is not sorry for asking you, but he is sorry for himself. He might have made bad choices, but maybe it was more just bad luck and he is sorry for that."*
"So what you're saying is he had some bad luck so he's apologising to himself on behalf of the world?" the driver asked. *"Damn I sure would like to talk on behalf of the world, or even do something for it. But sometimes, there ain't much to be done."*
The woman studied him. *"I think we can shape the world around us. With actions we can help mould the world for the way that we'd like to see it."*

He laughed. *"Woah there darlin', I didn't mean to get all deep. But think about what actions we as a species done did already. The world's full of tragedy and always has been."*

"We have happy history also."

"Happy history!?" The driver chuckled. *"Most of what we get taught is tragic history. Happy history isn't necessarily happy, just overdue."*

She shook her head. *"Not the stuff we are taught, but our history, our memories, our families,"* she paused for a moment. *"The house we grew up in."*

The land loomed. The light had not changed all day, it was a bright bland white revealing the orange and brown soil and the insects that worked and fought for food in the unforgiving desert.

After a while the driver glanced at her. *"I never meant offense by the way. As you might imagine I'm not particularly well versed in the art of discussion, I love this job but it sure can be lonely."*

"You have a family? Why do you drive so slowly?" She asked, noticing that the truck was well below the speed limit.

"Yeah, but my old lady ain't much a fan of me and my boy done grown up and jumped ship. Besides, I don't like to get anywhere in a hurry in this old steamer."

They sat at ease now. The day grew old and the insects scuttled into their nests after a heavy days hunting. The blue of night crept from the east and the woman settled to sleep awhile.

The sky cleared and when the moon had risen to its highest, the woman awoke with a start.

She looked at the driver, he sat steadily. *"You okay darlin'? You was muttering all sorts of babble in your sleep."*

She turned to look out the window at the blank starlit land. *"I have bad dreams sometimes..."*

He smiled kindly and said, *"Well hell, I barely dream at all these days."*

"I miss my town... This time of year, you could smell the cedars from the house. The olive and pistachio fruit grew green and gold." She blushed and looked at the driver as he pictured the scene.

"That's a pretty picture. In my town we got big grey buildings everywhere you turn. But I guess home is where the heart is. Ain't that what they say?"

"You're right, but some also say home is where the hatred is, I think mine is a mixture. Oh, sir, this is my stop."

The driver looked around, confused. The scenery had not changed for hours, the desert stark and eerie in the night light. *"B-but..."*

He stuttered, *"I can take you anywhere, this road ain't meant for walking this time o' night."*

The woman smiled. *"No road is meant for walking this time of night."*

"Please, you gotta let me take you somewhere else. How else you gonna get to where you need to be?"

"Thank you sir, but you might notice this place as similar to where I got on. Despite being miles down the road, I'm afraid I am no closer to finding my home."

Begrudgingly the driver helped her with the bag and wished her farewell. He looked around again, save for the altered light, the driver could not tell this area and the place where the woman had got on apart. He leaned to look in the passenger side mirror. Sure enough, in the darkness, a faint light shone through a window of what looked like a gas station. The woman had gone. The driver ran his hands through his hair, wiped the lonely tear from his cheek, then rumbled the old truck into first and rolled down the road, homeward bound.

Significantly Insignificant

WORDS BY Memo Brown

Who are you when no one is watching?
Who are you when time stops and your faith is lost?

Who are we? Who can you be?
Are you free?
Or are you simply
a result
a time sheet
a drum beat
a free for all
garbage sale
lost mail

What do we represent other than flesh and bones?
Other than Instagram and iPhones?
Why search for deeper meaning in such a shallow society?

Satisfaction

WORDS BY Abdullah

Human happiness comes with satisfaction.

Satisfaction comes with understanding that in everything you do,
belief is the best option and the right choice for you.

To understand this, you have to explore yourself, discover your
other options.

Then you will find your satisfaction.

[Un-title-d]

WORDS BY <u>Becksy Becks</u>

I am the proud product of Dr Kunijwok Gwado Ayoker and Mrs
Maria Nyadok Awang.
Both beautiful beings born and raised in the Upper Nile states of
South Sudan.
I was born in Khartoum, migrating in wombs as we travelled from
South to North.
Fathers, moving from villagers to philosophers.
Mothers, elegantly emigrating from housewives to ministers.
The wind span beneath wings carrying songs of midnight across
invisible lines and interlocking with tribes.
But as loud as freedom calls,
so too, does fall, the silent manoeuvres of oppression with every
move we made.
In every new step,
the old is swept under sandstorm rugs.
In every new breath, the stale smell of death seems to only
decompose in the marrow of indigenous bones.
Never in their own.
Darfur.
The first genocide of the 21st century around about two thousand
and four.
Where two to four hundred thousand dark black non-Arab men,
women children, slaughtered.
Systemic ethnic cleansing through the rape of mothers, wives
and daughters.
This continues all the way up until two thousand and now.
Refugee camps litter the face of this earth like flies on
hungry brows.
The spirits of a people killed in ice-cold blood flows through me
like lava.
Flows through these trauma filled eyes, whilst your silence cries.

When it comes to being a self-fulfilling prophecy, technically, your
inner perceptions should transform that world into your reality.
Try explaining this to a primary school kid, whose playground of
inner reflection stares back at a racist ring of roses.
Identity held hostage in a pocketful of posers.
Knowing deep down everyone is from the same land as you, but

only one in three looking back are anywhere close to the same
    shade as you.
It crushes you, cuts you deep,
so you remix your reality to play along with this game of Rock,
    Paper, Mirrors.
You figure,
if your heart of gold is locked away in a war filled treasure chest,
    what other reality can you expect to manifest.
We are an amalgamation of spirit and flesh.
Multi-faceted human beings that can multitask and navigate across
    narratives and multiple feelings.
Mankind has festered a society that plucks the lashes of hope from
    the eyes of the consumer,
and no sooner,
had my father fought for one Sudan,
the peaceful integration of Christianity and Islam;
in those final seconds of hope, is where my heart choked,
as it killed him too.

My river Nile has run illegal red lights through humanity.
Silence fell through open mouths during the atrocities of Abeyi.
How do we not yet have enough flower, to raise awareness about
    everything that is still going on today.

Every month my bank account stares into black holes that transport
    funds back home to feed those that are living in the red.
Every dollar I send home to mother she knows like the back of the
    hands that are used to build academies and house orphanages
    in my father's name.
Every shirt I've sent to swim across shores is for sure aware of
    every bullet that tears at its seams.
Every one of my donation packages sits at the shores of streams,
praying to a Jesus that it too can walk on rivers,
whilst fighting back the capitalist whips that crack quivers along
    its spine.
One day my DP may no longer be blue, but that's because my
    veins are.
Blue will stain my veins until my blood touches the cold air of
    this world.
When blue pics no longer exist on multiple displays, I find solace
    that I may still look to the sky for hope. There are several colours
    in rainbows created by my heavenly divine. You pick your lane
    and I'll ride for mine.

unapologetic

WORDS BY <u>Tinoula</u>

unapologetic.

someone, somewhere,
has taken their time to love a heart like mine, so unique, so fine in
  the eyes of whatever can be seen.
they have deemed me in a light of ethereal beauty and it should
  be my duty to embrace the being that I am.

I am... passion, the raging fire within me that cannot be doused,
  adding more rage to the fuse, giving my words meaning.
seemingly, I am lost, my medusa stare, colour too but sorrow in my
  eyes, none will see past my hardship, none see through my lies,
  hear my cries.

I am... pain, is constant, a constant reminder, an undertone,
  reminding me that my body is nothing but a warzone yet the
  shrapnel doesn't pierce my skin but bleeds through my heart,
  poisoning the parts that make me, me.
me, I say, presuming individually but how dare I say me when I'm
  like every other he or she that abides to society allowing them to
  dictate who they want me to be.

I am... flawed. an enigma wrapped in a mystery but despair still
  lingers on the tips of my fingers.
confusion erupts like a storm and identity is my sky.
constantly fluctuating lilacs and dark blues trying to find my
  designated hues but deadly sheets of black consume me.

I am beauty.
I forget stars remain even if they can't be seen.

I can't see past the future because I'm short sighted but I am who
  I am even when I'm absent minded but I'm not simple minded –
  I'm always keen to be enlightened.
all these complexities. the heart and soul are more than just words.
so this is for the words that were never spoken,
this is for the mouths that never opened
and this is for the hearts that were broken.

No more. No more silence.

I am authentic. I am loved. I am dignified.
I have felt loneliness to the point of isolation,
I have soared above my social expectation,
I am hate, I am fear,
I am the tiniest little tear in time embedding into broken lives like
    mine to spread hope.
I was there for you but I left you,
I am the echoes, the whispers of the words you were afraid to say
    but I am the shout, the tears of sorrow, the ordinary Tuesday,
I am a passing glance, I'm the shiver down your spine,
I am the taunting little voice, I'm playing with your mind,
I have lived, I have died, seeking redemption I have cried
I am me, but I am you and I see glorious technicolour too
I am the flicker of a page and I am so much more than my age.

I... am love. embedded into your touch and I know that it isn't
    much but I am the feeling of serenity and peace, treasured in
    your scarred hearts, tied together by bloody ribbons left by
    broken men, remnants of empty promises.
I am without you.
but I am not sorry, nor will I ever be sorry, for who I am.

Untitled

WORDS BY <u>Joseph</u>

Clambering.
Clung to a rope.
Brittle; sun soaked.
Wet with desperation.
Clattering up to the roof.
Neatly stacked in suffocation.
Early toil bled through to afternoon.
Fragments crushed under soul compression.
Staggered walks through permanent homes; squatting to
    prevent hardship.
Boats roll out and in, unaware of daily targets.
Conveyance.
Belted backs; hands strapped to carts.
Shadowed by another Euro-Orient oligarch.
Moss draped pockets covering crumbling stone.
Alone.
Desolate Island road, the forlorn drive with a refrained
    smiling stature.
Burning fuel to breathe easier, bubbling juices in charred shells.
Transient reflection queries.
Themselves.

Luminous foreign dreams unfold as steamboat engines
    happily scold.
Dim ambiguous prayer devours the day for an unknown trip
    from Oyster Farm Bay.

Medusa

WORDS BY Mahwash

Medusa
No one ever wonders
How medusa acquired her hissing crown
They assume she was born from the venom
Her darkness coiled around her soul

They never realise
She too was born innocent
Before she was tainted with tread marks and dirt
She was untouched like virgin snow.

Medusa dreamed like many girls do
With the naivety of youth
The promise of a life
Where she wore a crown embellished with love coloured jewels

Where her majesty was celebrated
Where the blossoms that spring forth from her mind are nurtured

And her seeds of intellect are able to bloom, spread out their
    petals and soak up the rays of another's affections

So soon was Medusa yanked back down to the dirt
To the earth the almighty created her from
Buried in it

Not as a way of nourishing her to grow
Instead, starving her of air of light
Of life

Before long, Medusa's crown of flowers withered
Desperate stems that once held the fleshy bulbs of fragrant lilies,
the silky red buds of roses and the delicate petals of jasmine
    flowers, slithered through the dirt
Thirsty, weak. Dying.
Desperately seeking the warmth of the sun to bring her light
    and life she willed these stems that once held on her head the
    treasures of her mind,

She willed them forced them to grow stronger, fiercer to seek her
　　sun, her air her life.

But the dirt.
It came by the tonne
Forever pouring onto her
Like the dunes within an hourglass
Infinitely spinning
No end no respite
No air no light
No life

Time trickled through her fingers
Like sand
She grasped at the nothingness for years
Never managing to wade out of the sea of dirt
With the promise of the shore teasing her on the horizon
She had motion with no movement

After much time, Medusas crown found solace in the dirt
It disguised its withered and broken stems
And was the perfect habitat for the snakes that grew in their place
Cold and wet
Suffocating

And so she emerged
Stained with the war paint of the clay she was made from
Birthed from the dirt that was thrust upon her
With her crown
Her army
Foot soldiers of her trauma
At the front lines
Ready for war
Vicious and hissing
Seeking her vengeance
.
.
.
.
.
.

They taught me
That the first name you hear is the lords and the last will be his too
But I learnt
Everything in between belongs to man

They taught me
You go from your fathers to your husbands home
But I've never known a home that papa lived in
And my husband was never my own.

They taught me
Crimson lips are for wedding nights and closed doors
But I craved ruby woo to stain my Cupid's bow

They taught me
Men eat first. First them then others
But my sister and I,
We stole meat from the pot to share with our mothers

The taught me
To silence your pain
That truth is a dirty word and your tears will quench the thirst of
    your tongue
But I learnt a mouth sealed shut
Will remain forever parched

They taught me
To cover my ornaments
Lest I lead a man astray
But I learnt
My body never belonged to me anyway

They taught me
That better to sweep it under the rug of honour and let dust collect
    in the corners of your soul
But I learnt that mutism won't stop my pen from bleeding upon my
    page and that leaves a mess not so easily cleared up

They taught me
To bear children would be bring me honour they would be the
    crowns upon my head
But I learnt they were my sword and my shield instead

They taught me
That tough love is not just an option but an absolute - words of
    affection are few and far between
But I learnt
To write letters to my children so they could read the words I never
    learnt how to say

And my children
My warriors
They hold together the broken pieces of my soul
String me together like pearls
Hold my heart in their tiny hands

And I will teach them
I will teach them
I. Will. Teach. Them.
Differently to how they taught me.
.

.

.

.

Titan
She is a titan.
She stands tall in the face of adversity
She is a soldier
She wears her scars like battle wounds
Each one a shiney medal
A token of her victory
Glinting in the sun
Her shimmering armour
God crafted her from warriors clay
Moulded her into a masterpiece
Beautiful
Elegant
The warmest of smiles
And sincere embraces
But behind the delicate beauty of her face
Behind the sparkle in her eyes
And the serenity in her smile
Behind is a warrior
Her war paint streaks her cheeks
Her eyes fixed on her battle field
And her weapon at the ready

And what weapon has god given his warrior?
What blade would be sharp enough to defeat the injustices
  ambushing her?
What barrel would be big enough to hold at bay the demons
  snapping at her heels?
God gave her a heart.
Not just any heart
A titans heart. A warriors heart. A mothers heart.
And as much as this world tries to take from her
As much as it tries to break her down
Brick by brick
Blow by blow
Shot after shot
She. Just. Keeps. Giving.
She gives away pieces of her heart
As if she has an Infinite amount
And endless well of love understanding and compassion
She takes the hurt
It disappears into her iron armour
Amongst smiles and solutions
And re-emerges
Something changed, evolved improved.
After so many battles fought
Foes conquered
Empires fallen
It's her turn.
Her turn to stop fighting
Her turn to be celebrated
Her turn to melt her golden armour
And where it as her crown
For she is a queen
She is a warrior
A soldier
A titan
And it is her turn for glory.

Hip Hip Hooray (Oh what are we like eh?)

WORDS BY Andrew

Hey you'll never guess what we've gone and done now
We've only gone and lost half our wildlife
How did we do that eh?
We're mad us lot, utterly mad, I mean we are bonkers.
- Oh what are we like?

I can understand misplacing a snake or two or even a gnu
I can see how we'd mislay a wombat, dingbat or even a cheeky fruitbat
It's not beyond the realms of possibility that we'd forget to feed a
rabbit (so easy to get out the habit)
But to lose half the world's wildlife
- Oh what are we like?

I mean I lose my glasses on a daily basis, these pesky specs
disappear without trace
I can tell they are missing because I can't see my face
I lose the flipper, the doofer, the watchermacallit so I can't switch off
the TV
But to lose half the world's wildlife
- It can't all be down to me

I checked down the sofa and there's no lost species there
No monkeys or elephants no tortoise or hare
I looked in the spare room for a Tiger or a snail
No swirly hard shell or long stripy tail
- Oh what are we like?

I looked in the garden but had no luck at all
Mind you it was difficult to see round the huge wrecking ball
The drilling was noisy and the abattoirs stank
The food hall was bursting and so were the banks
- Dollar up 10 wildlife 50% down

I listened for solace for silence for calm
But heard only white noise and the odd car alarm
I yearned for the Curlew or a White Fronted Tern
But they never appeared amidst the turmoil & churn
- Oh what are we like?

I lay on my bed but before I could cry
I was offered 5 quid for my tears salty dry
I rented my soul to a nice little man
Who pulped it and popped it in a bright red tin can
      - Oh what are we like?

So, as I drift down the gullet of this life and the next, I can't help
    but think that I should be quite vexed
But what do I care about people after my time, it's not as if us lot
    have committed any crime
To lose half our wildlife in 40 short years, it's just careless not
    wicked so let's raise three cheers

Hip Hip – Hooray! Oh what are we like?
   Hip Hip – Hooray! Oh what are we like?
      Hip Hip – Hooray! –
               What are we like?

What do we have

WORDS BY <u>Jasmine</u>

Enough food to waste –
Not enough to feed.
Enough money to spend –
Not enough to lend.
Enough land to build properties on
But not enough to provide a roof over heads.
Where have the priorities gone?

These cold streets leave people to suffer when they
Sleep –
A time where rest is key
But when can rest really start?
When all is left is a cardboard sheet
Under the bodies of civilians.
Where's the government to take action over
These dreadful conditions,
Of course,
They're just considered as an interference,
To the human race,
Just 'utter disgrace',
Let's replace them with skyscrapers and office buildings,
Forget the impoverished children just for a second,

NO.

How can one neglect the concept of humanity?
It's hard to have an understanding
When there's a lot of magnanimity
Within our society.
Creating personalities that begin with anxiety
Which proceeds into insanity,
Or those with the mentality of precious vanity.

You see,
The opposing lifestyles will always be in conflict
But, how about if you evict yourself from the picture
Just for a while
And identity the unfortunate with the same human being profile,
As you.

The weight of living

WORDS BY Saara

Too many days of our lives, we spend wishing we were elsewhere
Happiness under a cloudless sky, a million miles from home
Once we're there, we want to be home
Posting pictures of memories we'd rather forget
Scrolling through our phones searching for a hope we can't find
Dreaming of a life we can't afford to live
There's no state of contentment, we're always searching
    for more... for less
We have jobs we hate, friends we never have time to see
We live our lives constantly trying to impress people
But can I tell you something?
I'm so tired of all of this
The fake smiles, the attempts to please
Watching the world continue beyond where I stand
I'm tired of pretending this is perfect
That happiness is around a corner that I can't find
I'm tired of so much
But sleep doesn't help and I can't find an escape
I'm just so, so tired of everything

Lionel

WORDS BY Kate

There's nothing like a packed pedestrian crossing,
To remind you of just how big the world is,
Like the lady and her kids,
Who'll never know my name.

Abstracted Ambition

WORDS BY India Maya

Appetite liberates
trappings of avarice
Surplus pacify We,
earnest misbelievers
Bloated fancy, fast fashion,
and facetuned excess
The glutton ever hungry,
for the soul unsated

Reckless drones of desire
flatter only appearance
Drunk on caffeine,
anxious incoherence
Trinkets of corruption
brand the mindless hypnotic
Encumbered power
lost in search of prophet

When IQ plateaus,
sacred wisdom be known
Rule of logic mocks man,
for truth is juxtaposed
Heed the hour;
no freedom without restraint
For being imbued in all,
man must first reclaim.

ROCKS

WORDS BY <u>Jamiu</u>

keepers of time
our celestial prophets
watching in all its grace
mountains, boulders, pebbles
never wavering
in solitude
level
measured
still and quiet
yet in that exact stillness
it roars throughout the ages
louder than any cry uttered by
man, woman, child or beast
dances with the elements
revealing new layers
new life
yet
content
composed
composed
majestic in all its glory.

Excavating My Existence

WORDS BY Soloman The Wizard

I stumbled into Archaeology when I fell in my own grave...the sides caved in and I had no one to save my day so I gave in... My eyes opened to me racing up a landscape which...I'm sure I had encountered before but I had no time to explore because of the force chasing me. The law was gaining on me and I had no idea what I had done but knew I needed to run or I'd be...one... more...missing son...there would be no searches...only character besmirchments that would serve as another nipping in the bud... who would shed tears for the unloved and the scum? So I run... faster than I thought possible...the stones beneath my bare feet became my fossil fuel...turning...burning...churning at a rate far beyond the optimal and the beating of my heart became this horrible...thunderstorm...each boom in tune with the pitter patter of my scatter up these hills and the wind on my skin gives me chills...Have you ever felt the breath of death on your heels? At the apex I am met with a choice of direction with no seconds to choose...as these dark skies have now been tainted with unnatural blues that carry the hues of cultural abuse...a bruise on my hope of losing the fiends pursuing me...the siren song only accentuates my limited chance of escape...until to my right...I spot what would be my hiding place...a well that swells out of the ground like a mirage of safety...an oasis of shady dimensions that maybe be a haven depending on what lesson I am destined to receive...so I speed... the crunching of the leaves like the jaws of the beast...ready to feast on anything it can sink its teeth into...I tuck into the mouth of the well...

From my new home in the darkness, my senses are sharpened and the barking of hounds sounds like the harshest of judgements... more agents of Fear have been summoned to hunt up this beacon of Love...the thuds of my heart, an aggressively melancholy drum as this watery tomb embraces me in a farewell hug...Boots on ground sound around and above...hands disperse the Light and tug me into the shadows...the gnashing of saliva laced canines like poison tipped arrows...inducing paralysis as I lay below the gallows...and Death descends...raining down blow after blow... crushing the Life I thought I had known...the Hero falling to the Foe...crown spilled out and royal blood on show...

Although... a small glimmer of hope...my consciousness floats into words yet to be heard...crimson life force fuses with the red dirt and I once more reunite with Mother Earth...ready to be rebirthed...

I spend time excavating the remains of soul fragments the downpressors thought had vanished because they damaged the vessel that housed them...thousands of intricately shattered pieces scattered across lands and times I had once assigned no meaning and ascribed the feeling of loss to having no worth. It hurts... sometimes...to know just how much has been stolen but in this time of golden reflections...We find Our Soul's Own Treasures in the Blessed alignment of Self And Source. We call forth all of who we are and morph back into Beings of Days of Future Past and cast our intrepid hearts out into the vastness of all that is...constantly raising the vibrations of all who exist.

Declaration of A Survivor

WORDS BY Lucrecia-Seline

What do you see when you see me? Do you see the *one in four women* or *one in six men* that would have experienced domestic violence at some point in their lives? Or do you see the on average *two women* that are being *murdered* each week or *thirty men* per year?... Whilst we're here let me ask... Do you see the *four hundred* people that commit suicide after attending the hospital for domestic violence injuries? *Two hundred* of which do so on the same day they attend.

This information is hard to comprehend because I just can't understand how we so often let these people *slip* through our fingers. Including the flowers that are yet to blossom... Let me explain. *Thirty percent* of domestic violence starts *during pregnancy*, that's insane and inhumane! *Babies are dying* before they've even been born all because of a toxic bond that was formed.

Allow me to paint the picture... It might start with a simple hello, then they move on to conversations on the phone... meet up to take a stroll, they're on a roll. They fall in love with each other's character... Then there's a glitch, a sudden switch – His insecurities start seeping through the holes, bearing the true nature of his soul... He starts having problems with the time she gets home, like she isn't grown... Doesn't like if she takes too long to answer the phone and God forbid she answers with the wrong tone.

Then one night he can no longer hold the façade of his soul. He swings a punch that breaks her jaw bone and changes life as she knows it. She loses everything, her self-esteem cause he constantly tells her she's ugly. She begins to question her own sanity, because in her heart she knows that this is wrong but he tells her it's her fault... And he didn't mean to – if only she would listen then he wouldn't make the skin around her eyes glisten. So, she says sorry although she doesn't know what she's saying sorry for. This war goes on for years...

Confession...

These memories and flashbacks plague my mind at the most inconvenient times... I'm tired and growing weak. Unsure of how much fight is left inside of me... but *now* I relight the flame. This is not just a poem to entertain but *a declaration that* I, Lucrecia-Seline, am about to change the game. I am armed with magical melanin and a black magic cape!

It is time to break the bondage!

It is time to break the bondage!

IT. IS. TIME. TO BREAK THE BONDAGE!

NO PERPATRATOR IS SAFE!

Fuck serendipity

WORDS BY Chloe

We tell ourselves,
when things don't go our way,
that somehow it was meant to be.

But people will dance into our lives
and sometimes we'll never know why
they leave.

Dying embers of extinguished dreams
will dissipate as the ephemeral
beauty of smoke always dissipates.

Because sometimes things just aren't –
for no fault of mine
nor fates.

So if you're looking for *"a sign,"*
maybe,
just let this one be it.

Untitled

WORDS BY Katerina

I find myself wishing I had somewhere to grow old and mad.

State of Emergency

WORDS BY Natural

It's a state of emergency!
Our youth are living in 'Purge' city
The sirens won't stop
Mass losses from our crop
The street are running red
Too many sons are dead
Taken by the force of a blade
Or the heat of flying lead
Stealing mothers joy
She's lost her little boy
He's never coming back
She's trying to accept that fact...

"Where are you from my G?"
This cold mentality
It's like your heart is switched off
Conscience turn on mute
Can't hear it saying *"stop!*
He's just another yout!"
It's like your mind can't see
"I'm hunting down another me"
Your hearts can't be
Devoid of spirituality?
You've lost touch with your emotions
And your sense of humanity ...
This is insanity!

It's like you've logged into attack mode
'Black Ops' for postcodes
You're living 'GTA'
Each and every day
How did our seed
Become 'Assassin's Creed'?
The streets are filled with fright
Mass killing like it's 'Fortnite'!
You live on a 'Battlefield'
Where neither side will yield
Spitting, bragging, laughing

When another son has been killed!
Mama sitting in the 'Shadow of the Tomb'
Weeping; wailing
For the fruits of her womb
You play with life like it's a game
With no remorse or shame...
We need to seek retrieval
From this 'Resident Evil'
Stop the violence, cruelty and tension
You need blood shed 'Redemption'

How comes you're walking numb
With a knife or a gun?
Perception so twisted
Inflicting pain is fun
When did the dollar; that cake
Become all you need to make?
How did you become so filled with venom?
And with so much hate?
When did making blood run
Turn to something to be sung?
Death chant on YouTube
Stoking up each feud
Life has no value;
But you worship Giuseppe, Gucci and Loubs?
What's left you so disenfranchised?
Hardened and desensitized;
Branded; trapped; materialise;
So blood thirsty...
Murders are recorded, shared and televised!

How can it be so easy to take your brothers life?
When he faces the same terrors?
When he's living the same strife?
He's living with the same fear
Death is always so close, so near!
Those you are calling ops
You should see as your peers
You had the same dreams at primary
Both loved football secondary years
Rather than shedding each others blood
You should be shedding tears...

You're trying to fill your pockets,
Live your best life
But the for most...
It doesn't end living lavish
or with children and a wife
It ends in a box...
Where time slows and tick-tocks
Or buried... and time stops
It ends with you looking up at the sky
Screaming for your mum and asking why
When your taking you last breath
And your seeing your own death
Tears rolling from your eyes
Realising that you're really going to die...
But why?

Where are we going wrong?
Where has compassion gone?
Who hardened up your heart?
So your singing *"chef chef"* and *"chop chop"*
In every trap and drill songs?
When did your brothers death
Start to feel like nothingness?
As the death statistic rise
Do you harden up your chest?
Do tears fall less and less?
Can you justify your mindset?
Is there any reason left?
When did you start seeing your reflection as your enemy?
How long will this genocide continue in our community?

I said we're living in a state of emergency!
We need a remedy!

Untitled

WORDS BY <u>Lams</u>

When we cry,
We cry alone because they don't hear us.
We come to this country for refuge
Yet they fear us.
We are mercilessly murdered, but they won't help
Because they don't want to come near us.

Mothers are still crying
Because their children are still dying
Police are still lying
And playing duck duck goose with our lives.
We come here thinking we'll survive
Until another Shukri Abdi dies.

We are looking for answers that we'll never be able to find,
Because when it comes to our lives the public turns blind...

Why am I not hearing Shukri's name in the news?
They label our deaths as accidental
Even when the bite marks on our bodies are showing through.
It's not enough for our profile pictures to turn blue!
If only mama shukri knew...

If only she knew
That this isn't a land where the streets are paved with gold.
Whoever is listening to this
My advice to you would be to forget all the stories you were told

Because refugee lives don't matter here.
Heck, non-white lives don't matter here.
Now let me make this very clear...

We are disposable.
This position is non-negotiable
Because we can't negotiate the colour of our skin!
We can't negotiate the situation we were born in!
I don't even know where to begin.

Because these pages aren't enough for me save you.
You're reading this poem, but I don't even know if it will get through.
We are just pawns in their game,
Getting into the right positions for the blueprints that they drew.

So, my final question is,

What if it had been you?
What if it had been your mother's eyes that never cease to water?
Or, worse yet, what if it had been your daughter?

You would want them to say her name.
You would want somebody to blame.
You would want them to stop playing games
Because your life is not a toy!

Shukri's life was not a toy!
Yet, right now, her 12 year old body is wrapped in a gauze in
    her grave
While those bullies enjoy.

Flowers

WORDS BY Erica-Renee

It would be nice if we could be like flowers,
stand tall,
be surrounded by nature,
and appreciate that beauty comes
in all different colours.

Wildflower

WORDS BY Sophie

You belong among the wildflowers,
Where plateaus of hued green,
Overflow with dazzling displays,
And colours overthrow any shadow of pain.

You belong among the wildflowers,
I cried.
  I screamed it.
But the ugliest weeds,
Had begun to breed.

Colonising me, with seeds of pain and tragedy,
Their roots tore into me so deeply,
That if I tried to rip them one by one,
New weeds replaced them by the tonne.

Their sandpaper sides,
Slowly scraped against my insides,
So colours shrivelled.
    Dried.
    Died.
For any essence of life, to those weeds I was tied.

And then *it* came,
Surprise! Now frown!
    Good girl, you broke-down...

Too proud to swallow,
I began to self-medicate.
Sipping half empty glasses of liquid courage,
That's the lifestyle I chose to nourish.

And all too quickly, those weeds became my foundations.

Those fucking hideous creations,
Flared during dawn celebrations,
Manically laughed at all expectations,
I somehow... still managed to meet.

Find the case study that...
Glossy or matte?
Co-op dash.
On the lash.
Who's gaff?
Find the case study that...

Surprise! Now frown!
         Good girl, you broke-down...

Repeating this cycle,
I began to ask,
Is life really worth it?
Misfit, you're unfit.
         Just commit.

And no, I don't really have a sob story,
I was brought up in a family that was wealthy,
And I'll probably never know inequality,
Like our government's casualties.

But my brain was whacked,
Key pieces crumbled under attack,
So don't you ever say my cries for help were an act.
I was sick.
         Fact.

Days rolled into weeks and weeks into months, until in front,
     lied a girl I hardly recognised.

Who was I?
Dr Jekyll and Mr Hyde?
Being held under an unbearable tide,
By that vicious black dog?

Surprise! Now frown!
         No. Not now...

This time, strength replied:
Darling, beneath these roots,
              You can't dispute, that somewhere,
                        There's a seed for a wildflower.
And so I searched.

I frantically planted a thousand seeds,
Of love and kindness and good deeds,
So pain and poison couldn't proceed,
They didn't grow, I gave them nothing to feed.

Starved of the usual self-depreciation,
I filled gaps of damnation,
                              With admiration.
And those weeds went into starvation.

But my god, I'm not saying it happened overnight,
It was a bloody hard fight...
But no knight lifted me out that round tower,
And told me I was a wildflower.

I did.
In a bid, to forbid, those weeds from ever controlling me again.

And I've got to say,
Big up to my mother and brother,
And those who helped me recover,
Who always told me I was full of glorious technicolour.

Because when I began to also believe,
That I too belong among the wildflowers,
My mind no longer suffered from a hijack,
That made my roots black, rotted and slack.

Slowly, a delicate pink peony,
With the rich fragrance of frangipani,
An untamed waratah, bright as wattle,
All began to bloom full throttle.

And now,
I am carpeted by blooms.

And yes,
I'll always have a few weeds,
And fucked up philosophies,
But at least this wildflower got to go to some great parties.

Home

WORDS BY Naomi

Finally

I feel at home

But it's not a place

It's in my skin.

The skin I live in.

She

WORDS BY Sylvanna

She was tired. She had spent eleven years not resembling either of her parents but being told she had her fathers eyes. To growing into a woman who looked strikingly like her father. With thick lips and bold eyes, she smiled crazily, teeth and gums that could signal ships. When she laughed it sounded like a cacophony of demons, but still she was the most beautiful thing. With skin the colour of mahogany without the streaks of red and eyes like shiny pennies till the sunlight hit, that's when they became the sweetest brown macaroons. She was tired... Of her skin being the thing that people saw first, but still she smiled. She was tired of having to code switch and betray a tongue that didn't even know its origin to fit into society's mouth. But still she smiled. She was tired of her sex being weaponized by anyone with an agenda, but she smiled. She was tired of having to fight to be heard in rooms, where it was supposed to be civilised and supportive. She still smiled but she was tired.

For Love Alone

WORDS BY Bre

It was for love alone that I left the sea.
I wanted London to taste like cucumbers, gin, cold rain and hot
    Earl Grey.
I didn't think of the distance or what it would feel like to leave
    behind the sunshine.
Homesick my whole life, I am always missing someone
    or something.
Ten years in Singapore, six in Sydney and now seven here.
I do the math of my life and divide my heart up in it.

London at least is a city of people all from somewhere else.
In each others aches, we belong to each other.
To try and quell the homesickness, I wanted to eat like I thought
    an Englishwoman should.
My accent could give away my identity but what I ate never would.

I loved the pale creams and pinks, the palate of English food.
Rhubarb, custard, roast pork and beef with thick spoons of
    horseradish cream - they all delighted every plate I ate off.

I spent my weeks walking the city, mapping out the moods of the
    streets through food from the salt beef in Seven Sisters to the
    salt fish in Peckham.
Absorbing the new that would soon be so familiar.

I am a woman who wants to eat everything I miss.
I can't be with you, but I'll taste what you taste.
I cannot talk to you because of the time difference and I'll wake
    when you rest.
You'll be drinking coffee while I'm drunk on wine.
But we can cook the same thing and compare the weather.
Touch can be sent by a scarf in the post or through a lipstick that
    was once yours.

Living here I'm always waiting to go home.
I need the sunlight to soften my edges.
Wake up my freckles and set fire to my soporific sadness.

When I was a child I went to see a Swami in a hotel lobby in India.
He read my stars, told me Saturn was scared and to never leave
the sea.
But I did and the saltwater left my skin.

He told me not to leave the seaside so living here I try and
stay salty.
I smear tar-like Vegemite on toast, swish spoonfuls of soy into
sauces and drape anchovies over anything ripe.

I don't try and eat like an Englishwoman anymore, for what on
earth is one? I eat like a woman trying to remember all the
versions of herself.
My hunger is fed by heartache and home.

For love alone, I left and for love alone I'll return.
But while I'm here at least I know that seahorses sleep beneath
Trafalgar Square and a sprinkle of salt on something makes
it sing.

Wake Up Call

WORDS BY Adannay

Recently I've gone through a series of wake up calls,
Wake up before you lose it all.
Fall into my arms you can trust in our love;
Pain is a temporary feature of a brighter day.

I can't help but feel down,
when people around
think life just happens to you; that's not true.
When inspiration,
confrontation,
the freedom to exploration
allows you to explore your truth.
So, don't give in to the infliction
a habit of habitat,
imagine that -
we could be different away.
There are invaluable lessons
in a world based on impression.
Conquer anything with your mind and time.

Recently I've gone through a series of wake up calls,
Wake up before you lose it all.
Fall into my arms you can trust in our love;
Pain is a temporary feature of a brighter day.

So, wake up.
Take hold of your consciousness,
don't bow to your subconsciousness,
you'll find yourself consciousless.
Wake up,
grey skies won't lead to rainy days,
blue skies won't take away your pain,
so I'm gunna say again.
Wake up,
don't leave your fate to fate it's fake.
The power is within every one of us.

Pain is a temporary feature of a brighter day.

I want

WORDS BY Chloe

'And what do you want to do?'

'I want to create an event on Facebook to make terror in the streets. I want to live young, wild and dairy fucking free. I want to dance in a pool of uncertainty and oh my god, I hope she hurts me. I want to get bent over backwards all in the name of a small win. I want to eat like a pig all in the name of big sin. I want to see everything from a computer screen and hope my conscience stays fucking clean. I want to never hear you say you hate me, but it's not about what I want, it's about what I need and that's to keep myself from being seen, to be sad. Or happy. Or mad. Ultimately all I would have wanted is to have a good dad. I want a roller-coaster crash with a huge payout. Then I'll buy a semi-detached with no way out. I want a zero hour contract to kiss you goodnight. Then maybe this whole thing might just be alright.'

Breaking Borders

WORDS BY Sandy

Welcome to the world we live in: a border paradox.
While we are evolving beyond borders, digitally –
We are regressing by constructing new barriers, physically.
Seeking a break through.

Anxiety

WORDS BY Chevonesse

Anxiety feels like
the loud humming of a wasp that you can't see,

Anxiety feels like
catching butterflies with your mouth,
butterflies that reverse cocoon into caterpillars,
You feel it crawling in your stomach,

Anxiety feels like
a boxing match between you
and your breath,
the result either way is that you lose,

Anxiety feels
like rinsing your mouth with salt water
and accidentally swallowing a little bit,
it's the terrible taste of your own mistakes,

Anxiety feels like
Being trapped in a room with closing walls made of spikes,
floor made of Lego and a roof made of asteroids,
there is no escaping it's dreadful fate,

Anxiety feels like
throwing rocks at a wall made of rubber bands,
the harder you try to get rid of it the harder it hits back

Anxiety feels like
praying for sun after 13 days of rain,
only to open your window and see a tsunami of waves,

Anxiety feels like
being pac-man in a world with no power pellets,
just ghost,
no strength to fight,
you can run,
but there is no place to hide,

Anxiety feels like
trying to escape a forest of falling trees,
with no oxygen,
you cannot breathe,

Anxiety feels like smoking 20 cigarettes
one after the other in your bedroom on your own,
with your windows closed,
door closed,
Black smoke you can't see a way out, out, the trade,

Anxiety feels like
being alone in a space-shuttle
and hearing the panic buzzer,
buttons flashing everywhere,
no signal to earth,
you sit and hope that it stops but it gets louder
and louder,
you scream until the air around you occupies your lungs
till they explode,
Anxiety feels like wanting them to explode.
Anxiety feels like wanting everything to explode!

self-portrait as a microphone

WORDS BY Rebecca

sitting at a table
waiting for the flogging
what is the difference
between remaining calm
and functioning at a basic
        level
can take most of it
from gunshots
to dialogue
have no sense
of volume
but a thousand eyes
for classifying
how intensely I feel things
sweet
scared
these are things that can be measured
also the *timbre*
textures that are familiar or unknown

Where are you from

WORDS BY Georgina

Where are you from?

Where violence and war is all your familiar with? I hope you find a place to call home, where you can be proud to be a citizen of your new beginning.

Human beings are all equal, deserving of the same right to life. Humanity. Always. Before anything else.

He moves on

WORDS BY <u>Ajay</u>

He moves on...

The clock hits 7 in the morn. He could hear his Mom's voice saying
"*wake up! The breakfast is ready son.*"
English breakfast on the table with crispy bacon. Dad asked, "*is
your homework done*"?
"*Yes!!*" he replied with a smile mode on.
His brother started shouting, "*Yo bro! hurry up get your books in
your bag! And check if you got your lunch pack. And let me know
when you done... We already late for school, We gotta run!*"

There! Right there... he hears a truck horn.
That horn throws him back to the reality...
In the street... all alone.
It's not a shock for John.
For him it's just another day,
Engaging in food fights, begging money for his dendrites.
    But expecting something new when the clock hits 7 tomorrow
    morn... He moves on...

Like every day, he continues his street trip...
Instead of his mom's sweet voice, he hears a crazy car noise
Instead of him sitting at the table for breakfast, he find himself as
    a *hempel* sleeping under the temple.
Instead of his dad asking about his homework, he finds himself
    in litters, where security starts shouting get outta here you
    street nipper.

But expecting something new with tomorrow's truck horn...
    He moves on...

Voices

WORDS BY Mindful Poet

Trying to put pen to paper, as I sit down to write,
but with my own mind, I have to constantly fight.
That voice of self-doubt, that always seems to creep back,
any confidence in my own abilities, I constantly lack.
And this voice doesn't just appear, when I try to put poetry onto
a page,
I've had to live with this voice, since I were a young age.
Imagine what I could achieve without it, if I had a little more
self-belief,
that weight that would be lifted off my shoulders, with a deep
breath of relief.
But that voice is always present, it's constantly there,
forcing me to doubt myself, and to others I compare.
Where does this voice come from? I mean does everyone have
their own?
Even with a mind full of thoughts, sometimes I still feel so alone.
At times it's kind to me, and at other points it drags me all the
way down,
I might be smiling on the outside, but inside I feel the frown.
But each anxiety I feel can only exist, if I let that thought persist,
it's not about blocking out my thoughts, or trying to resist.
It's about accepting my thoughts, and acknowledging they're there,
and I have to stop believing that voice that tells me, it's just not fair.
Because we're all blessed in more ways than one, with every breath
that we breathe,
and if you self-doubt as much as me, then you need to tell yourself,
I believe.
I believe I can live my life, in conjunction with this voice,
I didn't choose to have anxiety, but how I react to it is my choice.
I believe GOD gave us all the power, to overcome depression,
learning to live with your own mind, is one of the biggest life lessons.
I believe this anxiety, is almost like a gift,
even when my body gives up, my mind puts in that extra shift.
So what I want to say to you, is accept that voice that's in your head,
don't let it bring you down, or fill yourself with dread.
Yes, at times it may fill your mind, with an irrational fear,
and it makes your vision seem that little less clear.
But it's a part of you, it makes you who you are,

and even if you struggle with anxiety, you can still go really far.
So pick your head up, keep moving forward, and keep working on
   your dreams,
because even living with anxiety, is nothing like it seems.

City to city

WORDS BY Luana

City to city
Mama can you hear me?
Oh this life wasn't made for me
Soft pits and astroturf quickly transformed into flip flop goals and
    bloody toes
Mama can you hear me?
This life is so sweet
Yet the paradox of sadness/happiness surrounds me
Bullets fly by while the sun sets
Saw my first desert eagle in a desert of what some may say is full
    of evil
So much power in an 11 year olds grasp
That's why I say Londoners are soft
Mama can you hear me?
I've seen life, flip to whatever chapter I bet you can't follow
As the rio flows and rats follow, me and the geckos have
    conversated, as long as we stay out each others way we good
Diverting streets filled with macumba
Are you still following?
I could of lost my mama AK to head
The disrespect
Walk in my havianas I dare you
Overstand the struggle I've witnessed
Tell me I'm mad for smoking this
Give me a reason
Donkeys parked at the red light, right beside the little boy selling
    stolen water for change, I left there knowing nothing would ever
    be the same.
More time in the gym wasn't needed, as hand washing clothes by
    the tank is quite the hand full.
Shit who knew my hands were so useful
I miss the days of flipping two mattresses to make a sofa or the
    times all we had was each other, things from London still on
    route so we sitting here with nothing to do, so we thought.
Rua 7 was the spot.
Cachorros quente, e hámburgas com palha, ice cold guarana
    natural pra beber when we were thirsty
Churrasco at the top of our road was a plus, copacabana beach

was a bus away living in a place like that it was so easy to stray
but we got told to stay away from the favelas but did they really
expect us to sit at home watching novellas?
More time rather be by rua 7 watching the fellas kick ball
Riding around the streets picking up empty caps for fun.
Internet cafes was the link up.
City to city mama we were so careless and free.

Age of the Strongman

WORDS BY <u>James</u>

Wearing a bicycle helmet, clutching a wooden shield, like a kid dressing up for an imaginary medieval battle, 16-year-old Dmytro tried to shield himself from the bullets. Out of nowhere, the Ukrainian security forces had opened fire on unarmed protesters. Almost 100 people were shot dead by snipers. Dmytro survived and his revolution succeeded, at least for a while. But for me it was a stark awakening about what happens when youthful idealism comes face to face with a ruthless authoritarian regime.

Travelling around the world making documentaries you see the best and the worst of humanity. And sadly, it's more often the latter. Recently, I've seen a worrying trend everywhere I've filmed: strongmen rulers playing on people's fears, creating a scapegoat for all their problems. From North Korea to Saudi Arabia and the Philippines, I saw the same pattern.

The first time I'd seen this was from the master manipulator himself, Vladimir Putin. In eastern Ukraine in 2014 I observed how Russian propaganda convinced much of the population that the revolution in Kiev meant that hordes of marauding neo-Nazis were going to come to the east and kill them in their beds. In a matter of weeks people who'd lived happily alongside each other, neighbours and friends, were suddenly so overwhelmed with fear that they no longer saw each other as human, just as a threat. I filmed this grim descent into what felt like madness – and civil war.

The next time I saw a society turning in on itself was in America. I went to Portsmouth, Virginia to make a film about a police shooting and found a town split down the middle on racial lines – half white, half black. A white cop had shot an 18-year-old black man coming out of Walmart at 7.30 in the morning. From lawyers, to eye witnesses, to jurors, they saw the event in a totally different way depending on their race. The jury in the murder trial was made up of eight black people and four white and was initially split entirely along racial lines – before they eventually did convict him of manslaughter. From what I'd seen, the toxic legacy of race still defined America – and what happened next was no surprise.

The film was broadcast a week before Donald Trump was elected; in large part because he capitalised on and stoked white people's fears of people who don't look like them. People need a strongman to protect them - and a wall, an almost North Korean concept. Once you start thinking of outsiders as less worthy than your compatriots, as people who 'infest' your nation, then it becomes much easier to treat them brutally.

We've just finished making a documentary in the Philippines. President Duterte came to power on a populist platform promising to wipe out drug users. At least 5,000 people, mainly the urban poor, have been shot dead by police in Duterte's drugs war. We filmed with the police as they explained their rationale for killing, with shocking honesty.

Surprisingly, even many middle class educated Filipinos support the drugs war. Duterte's propaganda has persuaded them that drug pushers are 'pests': a word you hear again and again when leaders are trying to dehumanise a section of society. People are all too willing to blame their problems, no matter how unrelated, on demonised and terrifying drug pushers. The reality is that the Philippines' drug problem is no worse than many countries and there is no proof that murdering low-level drug pushers in large numbers is even helping.

We live in unpredictable times dominated by populists like Donald Trump and Rodrigo Duterte who create scapegoats, whether they be refugees, black people, Muslims, or the urban poor. As our own UK politicians fail so spectacularly, people crave easy answers and extreme solutions. Worryingly, the time is ripe for a strongman who presents himself as a break with the corrupt old way of doing things. Having seen how quickly a society's stability and humanity can disappear, I have no doubt our complacency that this could never happen here is an illusion.

Kashmir bleeds

WORDS BY Maryam

Soil swells our
Souls, they sold
Ourselves

Watch

Our brains dwell
In bloodied wells, we overflow
The land

That fell

Our hearts are hardened, we
Scarcely live
Our bodies are fermented
We writhe in our
Deaths, we never seemed to

Ever exist

We'd be sitting one
Hour, eating one second,
Playing the next, a minute
Descends
Our necks broken

Dead

Cultural Identity Crisis

WORDS BY Hussain

I was 14 when I had a moustache
15 I hit the unibrow
18 coming home and the traditions of culture are asking me if I'm
ready to go uni-now

It was around 21 I reckon
Where anxiety weren't a question
I can't even love myself,
That's what happens when you tap out to depression,

Then you get the summers full of weddings
Where everyone wants to know
When you're getting married
Or if you're still moving on the low

But when it's community vs culture
There's certain things they don't know
And just because of respect to the elders
My generation

There's certain things we don't show

I call it moving

WORDS BY Mazin

I call it moving, they call it migrating
Life chances today, is what your tomorrow is against
Try to think about safety, about dying
Taking a boat to human rights
Choosing living
From just dying.

Ali from Kuwait

WORDS BY Softspoken

Ali was kicked out of science again.
And I should be surprised, or disappointed, especially when
I've asked him to work hard and, remain constrained.
How am I the only one who seems to see his pain?

I don't teach Ali.
But I see him act erratically in corridors and on the streets outside
    our academy.
Practically he's kicked out every lesson. I wonder how that could be
Until I met his mum and found out their situation domestically.

You see, until recently Ali and family had lived in Kuwait city
Living unfairly, indecently, in limbo, in their own country
Bidoon, stateless; heritage possibly Saudi or Iraqi
But it's all arbitrary. Ali's now just another student in a school just
    off Queensbury.

Thankfully his families asylum application has been
    processed successfully
And they have leave to remain in the UK indefinitely
But unfortunately Ali's dad is still working long hours illegally
And whatever free time he has is spent in shisha cafés constantly

So while safe and near future assured they're still stateless officially
But they've been evicted by the council and looking for
    housing frantically
Ironically back in the same situation they were forced to flee
And the school only found out when translation of Ali's mum was
    tasked to me

Tough cookie. Ali tends to fend for himself
And his honour is something he's always defended
But let's not pretend at the age of eleven he hasn't tended to
    address his lack of friendships
By using attention and humour in attempt to blend in

I'm sure that eases his tension. And who can blame him?
An accumulation of conditions has clearly left an impression

On a young soul battling bullying and lack of compassion
Frankly, assimilation fills Ali with apprehension

I step out and ask Ali in for a chat
Speaking Arabic no less to help him understand
Explaining to him my parents moved from Kuwait after they
   were attacked
Maybe - just maybe - he could relate to that

Next week Ali was kicked out of science again
Maybe I should be surprised or disappointed especially when I've
   asked him to work hard and remain constrained
But the pain he sustained explains why he's not all to blame

One of us

WORDS BY Washington

When I say one of us
I don't mean above anyone else
I just mean I'm brave enough to be myself
Searching and discovering, not scared to dwell
In my mistakes,
In my mental caged Hell
So I,

b r e a t h

a
n
d

e x h a l e

I try and I fail
I break anything that wants to hold me in jail
I read that book and I listen to that tale
And figured out the only thing holding me back is myself
So I ask you,
Would you like to be one of us?
Would you like to balance the light with the dark?
Would you like to be one of us?
Searching for the light in the dark?

I have a dream

WORDS BY <u>Siti</u>

I have a dream
That one day
People will stop the war in the world.
I have a dream that one day
People will stop discrimination.
We are same, we are human and we need peace.
Do you know why?
Because I always see in the news, social media and magazines it
    is all about war and discrimination.
I still remember I saw a boy sitting down covered in blood from
    top to toe,
Many people are suffering.
They don't have something to eat.
Walk from one country to different countries
Just to save their life.
Can you imagine!!!
If you or I were in their position
How would you feel???
I feel so disappointed, angry, sad
But I can't do anything
And I'm going to cry - really
It's breaking my heart so badly.
I'm very proud of them.
They are very strong
They can take all the pains
Again... again... and again
Even though it is hurting all the time
They lose families, friends and they even have lost the place to stay.
I'm really, really, sad.
I have a dream that one day
The sun will always shine in the world
The flowers will always blossom in trees and
The winds will blow through green and shady meadows.
Brother and sister
Tell the world that you are not weak
You are the strongest people in the world
Love and peace, that is my dream.

Revolution

WORDS BY Greta

The revolution has mid-heaven eyes
they have been staring down and blinking up
clusters of women holding hands,
their voices black, apocalyptic violet black
dropping land from their bibles.
They are part of an unremembered walk walking
that moves closer and closer to new ghosts,
new buildings in new rain, new languages
holding stories of abandoned bones
recording the last of the tree echo parts
the last of the exhausted red shadows
the last of suppression,
seasons, animals, mothers
blowing out low soliloquies of love
they have nothing to do with money.
A whole carpark of lights inside water
a whole heart of blood
resting on a whole heart of blood.
They have seen the naming of and renaming
of breathing earth that never leaves
but pulls at you harvesting
through the slipping dawn of daffodils
in prayers of freedom replacements wings
Geranium lungs ringing behind
classroom bedsheets of daytime
carried in the backs of vans
from one weather to another
the revolution is growing in your kitchen by the sink
crashing sky in the drains,
a throat of haloing eyes in the wind.

I was never the first and nor will I be the last

WORDS BY Tahmina

I am no longer planning to be number one.
I am no longer planning to say I am the first from my culture to do
this and that and this too.
I am no longer priding myself by saying I have taken steps,
crossed seas and am ahead in this race
when the difference between me and Her and Him and They are
of mere inches,

the spaces between boats. the spaces between one great uncle
gaining citizenship and now two generations later, his sons sitting
idly by, complaining about the ummah in the evenings because
bellies are now regularly full; and duas dreamt when hungry have
been answered.
So what do you do now when you've achieved all you thought you
could be?

I am no longer wanting to be the only one.
In White offices,
between polite pub conversations with girls, sometimes women,
who enjoy being at the top of the hierarchy trying to work out my
assimilation versus my relationship with God,
and because my ethnicity is currently cool, if they can win a seat at
my table.

I am no longer seeking to be alone. To be the sole representative of
all those mouths shouting for something different, when I am one
person, one heart, one soul, one set of palmed hands to pray, so I
am no longer celebrating myself being the only one on this stage

who looks like me. Photographs where one of 'me' in front of the
lens is *enough of me* to an audience that thinks and perhaps, *hopes*,
I am part of a trend instead of the global majority.

I want noise. Just like how I want the peacefulness that comes
from the privilege of just being, being able to be apathetic
and apolitical. How it's granted like the surety that comes from
accessing black and white cutouts of your lineage from hundreds
of years ago. TV shows telling you through public libraries who

your ancestors were, their marriages, their offspring, their butchers, their this and that.

Take a DNA test, *you can*. Your family tree is here and in one place. It's neat on White paper while mine is not just about suffering let me tell you— but dotted with the Partition, a colonial genocide that can never be apologised for and is yet to be claimed. Someone told your ancestors that they're Great, The Best, and everyone since has been retelling the same story, the good old narrative, and no-one has been taught anything different ever since. This is how inheriting believing-everything-is-yours works.

Instead, I get the questions, *oh if I had a taka for the questions*, assessing my validation via my contribution to society — or answering why my brother over here who has been able to swallow up the Syrian seas and not let it eat him up — should be allowed to have a home

When His home and Her home and Their home is marked elsewhere. And other.

When you say they are not *our* problem can you please educate me on the borders of 'our' and 'them'.

This mother tongue keeps crawling back up my throat to remind me but especially you, that I am hardly any different than those you scroll past on your timeline, the ones we all don't make time for, it shouts out that it could have been me,
it could have been my face in poverty, my ears listening to war,

my books burnt in case they were troublingly free

but then maybe I'd also get to walk around in places where I am the norm.

To live in a history, before it was erased, of writers and craftsmen and social shapeshifters, who did what we're trying to do, before me, and you and them. Before thinking we had to start from scratch, again and again.

I am excited for the day, where I can write about other things,

more mindless and fruitless than the politics of the skin. But until
then: I am them as they are me.

I was never really the first nor number one,
I am made up of those that came before, a tremble of what's
pending, a curve of what's to come. DNA synonymous with a
backlog of kindness, converted into resilience, *sabr* and sacrifice,
and those who somehow remained
soft and warm.
-

Alhamdulillah

The Brown Bee Syndrome

WORDS BY <u>Orin</u>

We are born of the Earth soaked in the blood of martyrs who
    lived and died for freedom.
So it's no wonder that the politics gene found its way into our
    DNA too.

But somewhere between the Sheikh Hasinas and the Benazir
    Bhuttos and the Indira Ghandis of this world,
Our manifestos never made it to Parliament.
Our campaigns never made it to the rallies.
Our votes never made it to the ballot boxes.

Instead
they were cast at home, more specifically in the kitchen
because that's where are Nanis and Bibis and Ammis found
    that their electorate paid the most attention.
Rotis and rice became the currency of power,
While empty thaalis meant a landslide victory.

You see,
our foremothers realised that the woman who
ruled the kitchen
ruled the roost
ruled the hungry men whose lifeblood came from the acrid smoke
    of that wood burning stove that choked our voices into the backs
    of our throats,
and the masalas we spent generations grinding fresh every
    morning,
with the pestles we carved from our very own spines.

So when our full bellied men went off to fight the good fight
    against the enemy at the border,
they left a warzone in their wake.
Turning Wife against Mother,
woman against woman,
our sisterhood taken prisoner and our shattered bangles as
    collateral damage.

But I was told that time heals all,
so I flipped that hourglass and tried to catch the grains of sand
hoping time was something I could bend,
fast forward to the moment in the movie where we would call each
other friend,
but I soon realised that while our constituencies can change, maybe
we women are destined to destroy each other in the end?

Yes we've moved out of the kitchens and
into the boardrooms, the operating theatres, the publishing houses,
so you'd think some things would have changed.
But our hatred for each other because of our hatred of ourselves
meant everything stayed just the same.
We must be some sort of masochists because when we love our
oppressors and fear our freedom,
Who else can we blame?

While as doctors we women have consecrated the anatomy of the
human body to memory,
created cures for diseases for over century,
but who knew our brown women politics would be so
fucking hereditary?

Our politics clung to us like a child to its mother's sari.
Our politics grew up with us,
no longer about satisfying those who could get their leg over us,
but those who could give us a leg up,
all while adorning us with gold plated shackles that we wear with
such pride
because our complexions look that much brighter when our wrists
and ankles are bruised with the colour of internalised racism
masked in the guise acceptance.

Forget breaking through glass ceilings
when you still fear cutting yourself open on my brownness.
Fear bleeding your own true colour
because no matter how hard you scrub you will always come off too
dark a shade of white.

There's a reason we can never the find the foundation that matches
the colour of our skin perfectly,
because they fear we might discover the richness we evaporate into
the atmosphere if we learn to exist unapologetically.

Fear that we might desire to be anything else but different versions
of alabaster, porcelain or ivory.

Forget the cries for representation when you still look at me and
    see competition
instead of sister or shared hardships because, obviously, the only
    way to uplift our communities
is to eliminate our adversaries
who,
funnily enough,
just so happen to look like
you and me.

In trying to breach the borders drawn up against us by
    white supremacy,
I refuse to let our brown women politics be passed down on in
    my legacy.
Elevating you means elevating me means elevating all those
    dreams of our mothers that weren't allowed to be.
We may have lost each other somewhere in this one-sided battle
    for equality,
but know this:
it is only when you stop hating yourself into invisibility
and dare to demand our liberty,
only then will we have won the wars that have been fought on the
    shores of our bodies for centuries.

J.A.M.E.L Outro

WORDS BY <u>Jamel</u>

My whole life I've had a chip
a massive chip up on my shoulder
but you know as I got older
that chip became a boulder
started to weigh me down
carrying it all around
left me with a bloody mental
like wearing a thorny crown.

I started asking myself
what really I got to lose?
What really is all the use
dying inside trying to fight
inner demons trying to prove
that I belong here?
They say: *"If you don't
know where
you came from
how you gon ever know
where you is going."*
The saying is true.
Although time is constantly flowing
that don't mean that your past
always has to define you
if you ever get lost or stuck
just.....
reroute

Star #401

WORDS BY Tarik

I wake up and the day feels over.
At night my eyes oppose my mind.
Bright lights like a supernova,
Everybody's turnin' up, but I stay sober,
I can't keep playing all these games,
Won the wars, but the battles bring me shame.
All food tastes the same.
One day, I'll rise. I pray.

Allah, give me the strength to
Stay to your path and stop me
When I stray. As days have passed
my demons laughed - I hope I'm not
Insane if I persist and I
Insist this mist will lift and
So I pray. God Forgive me.
Never let me drift away. I pray.

Looking down at all these faces,
So many people, so many different places,
Eyes on me, their books, their trainers,
Nobody got a clue how to find their way. So I
Light up the darkness with these stars,
As shadows seep through all my scars.
The crowds, still blind, wants one more chance,
But soon their future days are passed.

Nowhere to run, and so we hide.
The sun fills fools with static pride,
The moon (we're taught), will turn the tide,
The comet takes us for a ride,
The emptiness that creeps inside,
The restlessness as demons pry,
Nobody wants their love to cry, but
I have seen the signs! I pray!

Allah, give me the strength to
Stay to your path and stop me
When I stray. As days have passed
my demons laughed - I hope I'm not
Insane if I persist and I
Insist this mist will lift and
So I pray. God Forgive me.
Never let me drift away. I pray.

Allah, give me the strength to
Stay to your path and stop me
When I stray. As days have passed
my demons laughed - I hope I'm not
Insane if I persist and I
Insist this mist will lift and
So I pray. God Forgive me.
Never let me drift away.

Better than today

WORDS BY Rhys

I don't read the headlines,
I don't watch the news,
Cos I lose faith in something every time I do,
I don't mean to bury,
My head in the sand,
I'm just try'na live this life as best as I can,

Times get tough but I
Don't give up cos I
Know I'm not alone,

Cos we're all reaching for something,
We're all craving change,
Hoping tomorrow, tomorrow,
Is better than today,
And we're all searching for somewhere,
Trying to find a way,
Hoping tomorrow, tomorrow,
Is better than today,
Hoping tomorrow, tomorrow,
Is better than today.

It's not easy sleeping,
When I lay down in bed,
Cos I've got all these worries running through my head,
And it's hard to keep pushing forward,
When trouble pulls you back,
And you wake up even further from a dream you had,

Times get tough but I,
Don't give up cos I,
Know I'm not alone,

Cos we're all reaching for something,
We're all craving change,
Hoping tomorrow, tomorrow,
Is better than today,
And we're all searching for somewhere,

Trying to find a way,
Hoping tomorrow, tomorrow,
Is better than today,
Hoping tomorrow, tomorrow's better,

So just hold on, when someone breaks you,
Just hold on, when darkness takes you,
Just hold on,

Cos we're all reaching for something,
We're all craving change,
Hoping tomorrow, tomorrow,
Is better than today,

So let's keep searching for somewhere,
We're gonna find a way,
To make tomorrow, tomorrow,
Better than today,
Let's make tomorrow, tomorrow better than today,
Let's make tomorrow, tomorrow better than today,
Let's make tomorrow, tomorrow better than today,
Let's make tomorrow, tomorrow better than today,
Let's make tomorrow, tomorrow better than today.

The Winking Bags

WORDS BY <u>Amy</u>

I catch my reflection in the plate glass of the Prada store. My sloped back pitches my body closer to my phone. I need to go back to yoga. The glittering bags wink back in agreement. A week's... correction, a month's wages on a shelf. The work of distant Vietnamese hands. Pick and mix for the rich. *Do the sequins sailing in shipping containers care for 'port out, starboard home'? Do they know of the glass podiums that await them?* I pull my shoulders down and plough on.

I have allowed myself a detour through Mayfair – out of Green Park station, under the covered parking of the Holiday Inn, past housekeeping's furtive morning cigarettes, via the passage that sidles alongside the rare bookshop containing books I'd definitely never own and likely never read – because I am up early and in control of my life. I did not have 'him' in my bed. He did not mew for 'two more minutes'; he did not leave the iron on; he did not complain there was no toast. I will get a jump on those emails, write a neat list in a nice pen and be the strident, capable, professional young woman I am.

He is on assignment in some horrifying place, doing some dangerous and noble thing that makes me love him more and myself less. The smell of concrete and death probably hangs in the air around him. As I pass the fox fur-trimmed goose down coats dancing in every rainbow colour, I think of the taupe dust that probably coats his skin. I think of the sour grey yoghurt and flat bread pinched between his probably sleep-deprived fingers. I think too, of fox farms, pixelated videos and foaming mouth activists. *What exactly is polyamide?* As a florist with cigar hands heaves buckets of cut flowers dyed into neon oblivion, I think of a landscape desaturated of colour and probably soon, of life.

I have not heard anything in about thirty-six hours, but I have been told not to expect it. Communications are unreliable, the violent ideologues cut them off to isolate the people they terrorise and hamper those that try to stop them. Communications are unreliable, the coalition forces often cut them off to isolate the terrorists and hamper those that try to stop them.

As I pass the early bird selfie girls contorting their bodies in front of plastic pastel blossoms frozen mid-explosion around the entrance of a jewellery store, I do not worry. I do not worry because to worry would bind me to that old trope of 'The Woman Left Behind', all apron-at-the-sink and glazed stare into the middle distance of a suburban garden. I am not that and to prove it I had ignored a call as I boarded the commuter train just thirty minutes before. With the hot breath of a stranger on my neck, bosoms in my shoulder blades, I had worried only of my hangnail beginning to twinge, the sagging crotch of my tights, and of the creeping gap between my childhood friends and me, that we'd sworn on long vinegary-wine nights, overflowing-ashtray nights, would never happen to us but knew always would.

I have often detoured through this gilt maze, its streets thick with commerce, to see if my self-esteem can sustain another round. Another gut-punch. I tell myself I like the challenge, that it builds my resilience in a world that offers to underwrite and eradicate my emergent crow's feet, marionette lines and tear troughs at zero percent over twenty-four months. But in truth, I am a masochist. Today, despite the judgement of those winking bags, I am doing okay. The serious podcast in my ears reassures me as it discusses Global Issues - *you are just passing through* - and I relish the dissonance between the sound (illegal drone wars, the climate accord, Iran) and its setting (buffed brass, starched security, daily Windolene).

A call bursts into my phone, cutting off a pundit as they register their disbelief at the newly elected leader of the free world: Unknown Number.

I swipe right and breeze a hello.

He croaks. He is in a hospital. A bomb was detonated feet away. A house had collapsed. He is fine. A long pause, and then me:

"Are you joking?"

Another long pause; a forced laugh:

"No, really, are you joking?"

The conversation lasts no longer than a few minutes. He has to go, he is using a friend's phone, it is probably expensive. The newspaper would call me.

I am outside Salvatore Ferragamo now. I hear they have a new designer reinvigorating the brand. Kind of like what Michele did over at Gucci but more discreet. I was expecting this moment to be different. I was expecting the world to swim. I was promised that the ground would fall away beneath my feet, that I'd feel sick, that I'd well up, go weak, break down. The unbought white pelts and cashmere of the Burlington Gardens shopping arcade are begging to be part of this promised nightmare but the world is perfectly still. A radicalised youth with five tonnes of explosives and no hope, revving through the dawn streets of Eastern Mosul is not enough to shake me, nor can he make the avocado toasts that lie before the suited patrons of Cecconi's even vibrate.

The window decal of a chain lunch spot promises me health benefits, offers me variations on the Christmas dinner and pulpy lemonade. Eager tourists newly born to the city ask smoking gallery attendants: *"Tiffany's? Which way? Bond Street?"* Hoardings inform me of the 'considerate contractors' that lie within. Manicures and blow-drys and stale safety vests and takeaway coffee cups with leaky lids waft past me. Here, on this street, as the blood dries in the brick dust and acrid plastic catches in the throats of the soldiers too well to escape, I don't yet know of the future that awaits me. I don't yet know of the imprint the water glass will leave in the plaster wall or the sharp fragments I will find in my shoes months later. I don't yet know of the burn of the carpet on my skin, the afternoon lawyers we'll meet or how we will in fact one day put ourselves back together again. I don't yet know of his fractured spine or the fine grains of house brick just under his scalp that I will trace with my fingertips in the dark. I don't yet know of the friends that will come to rescue me, or the carbonara I will cook him to calm him down (just eggs, no cream, parmesan and lots of pepper). I don't yet know of the small talk, the heavy heart, the wide eyes, or the concerned hands on knees in darkened screening rooms. Here, on this street, as the far away twisted molten steel hardens once again, I don't yet know of the way we'll dart deftly from a discussion of our trauma to a: *"I'll have the Primitivo, I find Malbecs are often too dry".*

As I cross the thunder of Regent's Street, I barely notice but the podcast pundit has kicked back in. He is speaking of the impact this new era of American leadership will have on foreign relations. He is speaking of the terror that will form in us, and in them. As I open my inbox and begin to type, he is speaking of the atrophy that we'll continue to experience and the slow decline that lays before us.

It is my country

WORDS BY <u>Omar</u>

It is my country
It was the example of love
An example of peace and life

It is my country
A country where fathers laugh
Children live and enjoy
Mothers know what happens
Girls are queens

It is my country
School like a fanfare
Home is a haven
While you walk down
Smiles around you
Love everywhere
Kindness in every step

In one moment
One second
One day
One night...

Everything changed
Everything is different
Everything died

It is my country
It is like a jungle
It is a hell

Fathers are dead
Children are suffering
Mothers are crying
Girls are shouting
Schools are cemeteries

As you walk down the street
Blood is everywhere
Sadness in everything
Hopelessness in every step

It is my country
It was unit like a body
It was the country of community
Country of sunlight
Country of faith

It is my country
Where all the people used to sit and share happiness
Where all the people used to be together

It was my country
Now I don't know if this is my country
All the people are sitting and talk about using power
There is a young boy who lost his family
And there are young ladies who travel 30 countries alone

People are now talking about how many died
Now they are talking about sadness, losing and unfairness

Some people came
They cut my country in pieces
But it is not a cake

Everywhere around the world you will see someone from my country
Everywhere you will hear about the danger in my country

It is my country

It is Syria

Garnering Perspective

WORDS BY <u>Peter</u>

mother   land   father   land,
        home   land   home   soil,
home   turf   family   home
        family   history   cultural   history
National   history   colonial history
        colony   colonised   independent.
Outpost.
        Trading post,
        Cape   Coast   Castle,
castles overlooking rolling seas,
        parapets above dungeons,
        walls harbouring secrets,
        desperate etchings.
        A gateway.
        The Door Of No Return.
        Returning.
Look back.   Turn around.   Step forward.
Forward march.
        March on, with ancestral acceptance and blessing.
        Sing.
        Accept atrocities as our only history?
        No, that's not right.
        It's Hip Hop.
        To be a consciousness moving through history to re-attach
to back before
        (B)lack
        Extract only what is of use from pain.
        Alchemical change.
Repeat.   Maintain.
        Chill in heart of heat.
        Repeat   prayer.
        Repeat   refrain.
Lay claim to mother   land.
Father   land.
Home   land.
Home.

Motherland

WORDS BY Benny

I'm a child of the motherland.
Adopted by the West so that I could get an upper hand.
You see my parents, they always thought that in order to progress,
You need to live in the West, so their opinion was somewhat partisan.
They thought to get the cheddar and the parmesan
You had to be from the place that originated Arsenal fans.
Where bangers and mash was a delicacy you don't eat with hands,
And boy, if I greet you with my left hand, we can't be throwing hands.
It's that real.

But what was false,
Was the idea that the UK was a utopia.
What was false,
Was the idea that the UK was a Garden of Eden,
Where the streets were filled with gold whilst we all walked
    with freedom.
Because in reality,
The streets are just filled with pennies and coppers or coppers and
    chewing gum.
But then I guess,
I guess I would rather walk in a place where the streets are filled
    with coppers and used gum,
Than somewhere like America where the streets are just filled with
    coppers that use guns
Particularly on a demographic with a darker pigmentation,
But that right there,
That's another conversation.

Because you see what pains me?
What pains me is going on BBC and ITV
And seeing news of another 'IC3' or an 'RIP'
Because when I look into that box, I see the reflection of a person
    that looks
Just. Like. Me.
So you can see that it physically burns me
When the media and the press just give it the third degree
Despite the fact that there's people that look like me in uni's trying
    to work to get that first, second, or even third degree.

You see for a long time,

For a long time it was hard to be from the motherland.

But now the children of the motherland can walk with their fists up
and have the upper hand.

The game is the game but we're the players that are changing it.

I'm talking Sport Stars and Superstars,

Lawyers and Doctors,

Entrepreneurs and Engineers,

There's a change in the atmosphere - And can you smell that?

That's the smell of young Kings and Queens walking through this life

Smelling like,

COCOA BUTTER AND SUCCESS –

Get used to the stench!

We have the foundation to impact future generations.

We can fulfil the hopes and dreams of ancestors that went through
forced or unforced migration.

Because not all superheroes wear capes.

In fact I know a couple superheroes that wear kente.

And pele I forgot about my Nigerian friends

Because they know a couple wonder women that wear gele.

See I'm talking about the mums and dads, aunties and uncles,
grandparents,

That have fought, sacrificed and worked with a work rate like
N'Golo Kanté,

So that's why I'm telling you, be inspired by your roots as if you're
the descendants of Kunta Kinte.

So here's some food for thought from Warren Buffet.

He said, *"Someone is sitting in the shade today, because someone
planted a tree a long time ago."*

Denzel Washington also said, *"Don't just aspire to make a living,
aspire to make a difference."*

So what seeds can we sow to help someone blossom, fly and shine
into a better tomorrow.

Because, *"with great power comes great responsibility."*

You might know those as the words of the uncle of Peter Parker,

But I envisage that as the actions of Kwame Nkrumah.

Because when Ghana got independence he said, *"We must set an
example to all Africa."*

But this is a new generation and we can set examples to the whole
   world because,
We are a new breed with a
Whole. Different. Calibre.

So like I said, I was born in Britain
But I'm a child of the motherland.
And now the children of the motherland,
Should walk with pride like how no others can.

Be proud.

Home

WORDS BY Kavita

In the end have realised this.
In exile or forced to leave you
Imagine the agony suffered by me
Our flesh and blood, our kith and kin
Suffering, in the name of religion.

This is the first verse of a poem written by Raj Daswani, expressing the pain he still feels that he, a Hindu, had to leave Sindh province, over seventy years ago, when it became part of Pakistan. Religion was the reason for the division of the Indian subcontinent in 1947. It created millions of refugees as Muslims fled to Pakistan, Hindus and Sikhs to India. It is the largest migration in human history outside war and famine. Raj lived with his family for years in a refugee camp in Bombay, before moving to Britain. He still feels a visceral, powerful attachment to the land of his birth. When he finally returned for a visit to Karachi in 1992, the first thing he did was kiss the ground, saying *"Mother, I have come home."*

This connection to the land that partition refugees were forced to flee has endured for many, even though they moved to a new country, and then migrated to Britain. They remember with great clarity how in an instant they quickly packed whatever they could before they fled: a spinning top, a favourite book, a piece of jewellery. Many thought they would soon return once the initial trauma of partition subsided. Not one did. Homes, friends, keepsakes never to be seen again. That does something to you. What you think of as home, is not home anymore. Your history there has been erased. The knowledge that things can change quickly doesn't leave you. It gets passed down through the generations. The imaginary suitcase at the top of the wardrobe in case you have to move again.

Of course you can rebuild your life, and make a good life. But the generation that was forced to flee never forgets. Many wanted to go back one last time before they died, to see the tree they played in as a child, visit a parent's grave, or glance at the home of their birth. The mythology of the place you and your ancestors are from - *desh* - survives down the generations. Home comes to mean many things: the place you are originally from, the place you were forced to move to, the place you chose to migrate.

Raj Daswani took with him some stones on his last visit to Karachi. He keeps them in his study in London. It is a tangible reminder of the place he grew up. He takes them out carefully, and puts them to his lips and kisses them. *"It is as if I am still connected to my soil."*

My identity

WORDS BY <u>Nomusa</u>

My identity used to be the blurred lines you see when you forget
   your glasses,
Or maybe it was broken glass unswept after last nights argument.
The urge to fit in, as I forget who I really was, ate me up inside.

African child where?
That was not my identity.
I was just British.

I tried to fit in with my friends.
I despised my hair.
My skin used to make my gut churn.

African child where?
That was not my identity.
I was just British.

one history lesson changed my whole life
empowered my whole atmosphere

African woman. YES!
Now that's my identity.

I began to love my afro hair
Smile at my Melanin skin.

African woman. YES!
Now that's my identity.

Words

WORDS BY <u>Simon</u>

Like arrows in quiver
Discerning to deliver
Delicate touch
Means so much
Precision in decision
Avoids harmful collision.

Fiery arrows; pierce heart
If not careful
They will tear it apart
Detecting your 'stop' and 'start'
Now becoming a delicate art.

So many words you feel to say.
Grace. To hesitate. To Pray.
Wisdom knowing.
When to save for another day
Don't find yourself lost in grey.

So don't be naïve,
No excuse in trying to leave
You know what you believe
Not one to wistfully weave
No pretending to conceive
That is truly to thieve.

Learn now... to just breathe.

M.A.N.

WORDS BY <u>Tommy</u>

i'm mean with the pen
what does it mean to be men
is it the vocation on which our self-esteem depends
perhaps it's a hipster
on the scene leading trends
is it the lead in a Hollywood romance
a road man
balling in a Beemer or Benz
once seen in the ends
now spending fifteen in the pen
scheming with dreams of revenge
escape to victory
football season again
sat round a screen
cussing the other team with his friends
but are our relationships
just a means to an end
be it work
or social life
socialising over pints
at open mics
riding motorbikes
repairing broken lights
but broken hearts are hard to fix
i'm asking if
married men live longer
do bachelors die younger
from a lonely life
that's cold as ice
now I've broke the ice
don't slip
but us blokes are prone to oversights
husband didn't notice wife's new hair cut
doesn't he care much
I don't know
we're all unique
don't compare us
it's essential

I don't essentialise
across gender lines
or generalise
but do the general public
genuinely think strength resides
inside a gentle guy
paint the canvas
rap artists portraying gangsters in songs
the stronger guy can tame his rage and anger
less Incredible Hulk
more David Banner
minus the rays of gamma
flashing lights like Kanye
Westerners clamour
for fame and glamour
enamoured
but afraid to say I love you
so we engage in banter
evasive grammar
but I parley with candour
speaking truth to power
more than waving banners
Che t-shirts
car stickers saying save the panda
guys: cherish your pride
lionesses raising Panthers
a Lion King's never too proud
to change their pampers
and they ain't pampered
or afraid to stand up
like Huey Newton or Gil Scott
the revolution will not be televised
but we still watch
Beyoncé and her dancers (formation!)
it's also Tommie and John on the podium
opprobrium
cause they raised their hand ups
when we raise our hands up
it's in raves raising champ up
want to raise a champ up
man up
raise your standards
the way my stanzas are packed with imagery

they might not grasp my similes
but they can't say I lack ability
so I'm damn good
what's manhood
i want to ask officially
is it a social construct
we enact from infancy
or is it innate in our capillaries
is it a vain metrosexual
attractive physically
is it a captain of industry's unmatched efficiency
the epitome of an alpha male
too tough to ask for sympathy
is it Beethoven's crashing symphonies
is it Stormzy clashing lyrically
is it Einstein's intellect
gone past infinity
what's passed is history
there's joy after misery
I'm just one man
trying to master
masculinity

Open Mic

WORDS BY Elan

Open mic
Open hearts
Open light
We openly cry when the truth
Is spoken into the lies
That we've become acclimatised to

Koz sometimes it does feel like
Society denies our right to be united
But with the flow of poetry we ignite
and fight through

Spitting fire from our burning pain
Sparking up a conversation on the burdened shame
Could be nervous at first
But through the exchange
Learn our personal hurt
Has a universal claim

We're revealing human nature
No longer aliens
Discard the spaceships
We been sailing in
And start to make this
Room a haven and
Light the dark and gloomy spaces
In our hearts...

Like when I witnessed
A homosexual Muslim woman
Rhyme about the fight to be loved by her parents
Her bravery in sharing left me disabled
From hiding behind my heterosexual atheist labels

The night was abundantly caring
As she poured out her demons
And tore down the seams of my I.D
She made my eyes weep

For the right to be loved by her parents

And I'm there thinking,
"Woah!
I'm not ready yet"
Then the verse got heavier
And the words were Hediyeah
But I felt it in my soul

As the story she told
Began to mirror my colder moments
In becoming a grown up
Tears flowed up and rolled down as she
Rolled out this vision of life in an alternate reality
Where people could understand and see her
For the person she happened to be

Now I'm sat finger snapping and clapping
Some bredda in the back is just brappin'
As she's attacking each stanza, landing punches
A labour of love, I got my hands up
Bout ready to stand up and erupt
Koz she's abruptly interrupted
The mundane corrupted way
We live day to day
But thing is
Wait

I have to say,

Though the night was unforgettable
It was far from unique.

Koz all throughout the city, every week
From the haven in these pages
Translated to speech
Poetry provides a sanctuary

People step up to these platforms and speak
They reach us and teach us
To breathe and be free
Koz we need love

We seek hugs
And deep unity
We are human you see

Open mic like fresh air
When you arrive at the beach
Yet it's the tide, it's the sea
The undeniable need to be
Swept up and released from the plastic presentations
We perform on the streets

So come to share
Come to be
Come to bare
Come to breathe

Whatever your story, whatever your fight
Write it, share your plight
You'd be surprised with how many
Like minded lives you find
Once the labels we cling to are set to the side.

Feed The Meter

WORDS BY Sadie

They called us Jam Families
J.A.M.
Just About Managing.
I'm at the head of a hungry jam fam.
I'm in a jam, man.
I'm in a stew, I'm in a jam, I'm in like a lion, out like a lamb.
Fat gets chewed like smoky ham,
So bring home the bacon, bring out the Branston,
Crusts make curly hair so handsome.
Drip feed easy meat, feast your eyes on all you can eat.
Eat like a pig, eat like a bird, eat your heart out, eat your words.
One bad apple far from the tree, cheap as chips and chalk
    and cheese.
Bite your lip and bite your tongue and dish the dirt on the bun in
    the oven.
Running around like a headless chicken, take the heat – or get out
    of the kitchen.
Sugary spice and all things nice, frugality sticks like white on rice,
Sugar coated sugar daddies cash is stashed in old tea caddies.
Dog eat dog, dogs dinner, done up like a Sunday kipper.
Piece of meat – there's no winners; sinner, sinner, chicken dinner.
Meat head, meat wagon, two veg, how did it happen?
Crying over milk that's spilt, poor nutrition: mothers guilt.
Cold turkey, dead meat, eat to live not live to eat.
Gone belly up with your last belly laugh, this dogs bite is worse
    than its bark.
Brown sugar, brown bread, bread of life but close to dead,
Cast your bread upon the waters.
Dish of the day like a lamb to the slaughter.
Couch potato: Loafing about but still wants a meal that melts
    in the mouth.
Bitten off more than he can chew, but we'll have it easy-peasy soon,
With the food of the Gods in a greasy spoon.

Never put all your eggs in one basket: we need to be fed but we
    don't want to ask it.
Wish it could be the other way round, but this slice of life falls
    butter side down.

Man's got a job and he still can't eat: choose between rent and
    food and heat.
Poverty porn and bread and circuses, forlorn looks from
    social services.
Don't think less of me, empty soul, I've got a recipe best
    served cold.
My army marches on an empty tummy to a land of milk and a land
    of honey.
A land sold out of humble pie where no one asks stupid questions
    like *"Why?"*
We drink and be merry rather than cry when cupboards are bare
    and cold and dry.
Pat-a-cake, pat-a-cake, bakers man, bake an escape as fast as
    you can.
Cook my goose or cook up a plan as I've used up tomorrow's jam.

Need more ballast? Empty freezer
Caesar salad, tastes that tease ya,
Feed a cold or starve a fever?
I can't work out this one either:
Food for thought?

Or feed the meter?

Pen to Paper

WORDS BY Nathan

It's not aimless trying to be famous
Go out there and chase your dreams
Don't let a social construct take our teens.

In a world filled with robbers, tax dodgers, and political bothers.
It's pointless chasing ratings, combat with your fingers; mind over matter.
Pen to paper; Educator.

No two journeys are ever the same,
Some come showering with glory
Some come stricken with shame.

A Parliamentary candidate
A happy, light, refreshing matinée
A meeting or a frequent 5* holiday.

A concrete jungle, a 3am royal rumble.
Creativity flies to mind; for I am creative just like you.
Hidden in the shadows of the plainest views.
I speak creativity not just for I but also for you.

Bitter World

WORDS BY Ally

Who cares about the people running from the dark
Who cares for the soulless searching for that spark
They're all alone, waiting for someone
What happened to the rainbows, after those storms
What happened to the friends who were supposed to mean more
We seem to ignore, but oh, we broke them

White T-Shirt

WORDS BY <u>Remington</u>

They say love is clean, they say love is pure
I say love is like a white t-shirt we buy from the store
Find it anywhere from Primark to Dior
You find love anywhere from abroad to next door
A dirty white tee you don't want anymore
A person that cheats you can't handle anymore, wash your t-shirt,
    tryna get it clean
but
The stain remains, pain the same in love once it stained it wouldn't
    be the same
Tryna change the tee for something new
Tryna look for love in places you never knew

Love, is it clean or pure?
Is it me and you?
We keep on falling in love
No matter when things get rough
You never give up on us
You leave me waiting around for you to get home
So high am, feeling like ecstasy
You got me, so mesmerised I don't want it to stop
I can't let, go of your love I don't want it to stop
So high on, loving you

They say love is clean they say love is pure
I say love is like a white t-shirt we buy from the store
Find it anywhere from Primark to Dior
You find love anywhere from abroad to next door
My crisp white tee it feels so clean
I got her talking in falsetto like I was the dream
How much your tee worth how much you buy it for
Put a value on your love. Is it rich? Is it poor?
Longline over size tight fitted tee
Love comes in different ways
So when it comes your way
Stay strong not weak like seven days

Time

WORDS BY Shamaila

Time cries silently when first born.
It tells a tale,
Accompanied by us,
Yet dies living alone.

And I guess -
We
Repudiate time as a paragon of perfection.

We belittle it, mock it, scorn it; yet it laughs at our naivety.
It lives mourning for us -
Everyday, every second.

Time cries.
Why?

We are a generation
Which walk the same paths of
Those who helped birth beginnings from many ends.
The same paths,
Where the foundation of their identity was challenged.
They were disregarded, dismissed and defamed.
Yet they remained still, grounded to their roots, becoming the
    authors of their triumph.

Time cries
As it ponders,
Why we tend to forget that we are composers of
Our victory,
Our success and our greatness.

Time cries
As it patiently waits for us
To birth our beginnings,
For us to unlock the power within, to flourish, grow and blossom.
It is time we nourish and revive our souls,
And awaken ourself from the sleep of heedlessness.
To proudly and finally,
Claim and save
Us, you and me.

Serenity

WORDS BY Ellie

Serenity,
Apart from it's not serenity,
It's drinking four bottles of sweet wine in a rose petal bath but still
    feeling empty,
Like you're just a mirage and the liquid soaking your translucent
    skin flows freely from the glass neck,
The colour of blood but yours isn't the same,
Yours is heavy layers of dust off of Grandma's clichéd china pieces.

Emotionless,
Yet feeling the weight of your life and 7.6 billion other people's all
    at the same time,
Crushingly freeing,
Dragging you down and catapulting you far into the stratosphere,
Where there is an abundance of oxygen yet still feeling your
    withered fingers clawing at your throat,
Begging for you to take your first breath.

Serendipity,
That you're the one drowning in idle sorrow whilst she is living
    in utopia,
But wondering why you? Because it was her that caused this,
Now she's constantly laced into your subconscious fear that
    nothing will ever be permanent in this universe,
Yet she's still the accidental light of your life as you drive past every
    piece of what was once her,
Timeless memories that stop time in your ever-ticking, overflowing,
    24/7 mind

Restless,
Your brain is a jumbled mess of nothing making sense,
A visibly tampered-with time-lapse of people buying too much
    dated 'medication' on loop (and then rewind),
Like a constant reminder that people are free, but habits are not,
And her die-hard, soul-crushing, whirlwind habits just happened
    to rip your world into shreds of self-destruction and
    abandonment issues,
Only to be eased with remaining friendships grinded into almost
    nothing and smoked in a hazy room.

Belonging

WORDS BY <u>Lynn</u>

It's when I go through passport control that I feel like I am home. In other countries, they're rude at passport control. But where I'm from, they're nice. Perhaps it's because I'm from there. Perhaps that's why they're nice to me.

Perhaps not everyone, from everywhere, gets the cheery *"Welcome!"* delivered with a smile. Perhaps the immigration officers don't read out everyone's name as part of their welcoming salutation.

Maybe they only do that for me – and people like me. Maybe some people go through passport control and they don't feel like they belong. Maybe they're made to feel like they don't belong.

I pick up my suitcase from the luggage carousel and I walk out into the air, which is usually colder than where I've come from, often wet with drizzle. I contemplate getting a bus but I nearly always get a taxi. The airport isn't far from where I'm going, I reason, as I watch the meter run.

I spend the weekend among my family or my friends, celebrating something: a new baby, or a summer wedding, or Christmas, which gives us an excuse to eat and drink and bicker. It's often joyous, even the bickering, and that makes it difficult to contemplate leaving again.

I consider staying. Maybe it would better here: more relaxed and friendlier – it's not only the immigration officers who are nice to me, everyone is. The people in shops smile when they give me my change!

I visit places that I used to visit when I was younger. I see a hotel and I remember going to a disco there one summer 20 years ago.

"That hotel has been turned into a direct-provision centre for asylum seekers," somebody tells me, as we walk past. *"There was a lot of fuss about it, from people in the town."*

I think about those asylum seekers – what they've fled in that old country, what they have arrived to in this new country. But then I go to the fishmonger and cook linguine with clams and gossip with my sister and I forget about the hotel and the asylum seekers.

After a few days, it's time to go home. I get on a plane and go back to where I came from.

I am lucky that this is my reality, that I feel at home in two places. The ease with which I can travel and live and work in two different countries makes me among the most privileged on earth; plenty would risk their life for what I've got.

If the conservative government gets its way, people like me – younger versions of me – won't have this life, they won't feel at home in two different places.

And if more and more people are made to feel like they don't belong here, like they aren't at home here, I'll feel less like I belong here, less like I'm at home here.

I get the train, then the bus, back to my flat. I send a message to my family to let them know I'm home safe.

I remember that hotel, once plush, now less so. I remember the asylum seekers and I feel useless.

Then I forget them again. That's what happens, that's what we all do, all of us who consider our belonging a right. All of us who have been told that we belong, always will.

Humanity

WORDS BY OT

Humanity is like the wind, inherently free and untameable, it grants life but can be ruthless in destruction,

Humanity is capable of the epitome of kindness, but can be the cause of the utmost of pain,

Humanity knows no boundaries, no gorge as deep, no cloud as high as the possibility or rather probability of our potential, but still we are infant like in the manner we destroy, inflicting ourselves upon each other and our Earth,

Humanity is social, but so often alone as we squabble for hierarchy and material in the caverns of the shallow whilst neglecting to recognise our rightful position in the world of the infinite,

Humanity is as nature herself, wild and unpredictable yet nurturing and ordered with divine design,

Humanity is polarity, love and hate, joy and sorrow, ecstasy and depression,

Humanity is human, that is to say perfectly imperfect, woven from the very fabric of the volatile universe itself,

Humanity is both lost and found, shrouded in darkness yet immersed in light, we hold the key to our future but are poisoned by the lure of the inner temptress that wills our demise,

Humanity is individual, formless and without any one definition, humanity is the most prominent expression of liberty conceivable, no bounds or labels can be fastened to that which is so free, so fluid and alive, so bestowed with celestial conscience,

Humanity is you, humanity is I, humanity is us, humanity is to celebrate our differences and stand unified in the name of that which we all share, that which is beautiful,

Humanity.

GLOSSARY OF STORIES

The humans behind the words

Contributors

Salah Shigaf *p.10*
Salah Shigaf (pictured left) is a 25-year-old refugee from Sudan. Salah grew up in a small village without electricity, water or mobile service. He took care of his family's cows and enjoyed playing with the other children under the moonlight. At 11, the Janjaweed militia attacked Salah's village, killing the people he loved and destroying his home – he refers to their killings as genocide. Salah was trafficked and forced to work in Libya (*"hell on earth"*). He escaped and travelled to Europe by a boat - which ran out of oil mid-Mediterranean. Many people drowned, but Salah was saved by a ship with a British flag. As an intelligent young man, Salah now studies at university and loves reading and dancing. Salah is one of Co-Founder Sophie's dearest friends and was the original inspiration for the Words By project. *"Sometimes I feel bad. But it is ok. Just remember. I am human too..."*

Lateshia Howell *p.11*
Lateshia Howell trained as an actor at the Guildford School of Acting and graduated in 2017. Towards the end of a six-month UK-wide Shakespeare tour, she turned to writing poetry as an outlet from her hotel rooms. After finishing the tour, she started going and performing at Poetry Open Mic nights. Since then, she has appeared on BBC Radio, headlined her first spoken word show and been selected to go on a poetry exchange in Scarborough, Canada. Lateshia recently decided to take a year out of acting to pursue full time charity fundraising work, in the hopes of travelling around South America. She wants to become charity poet, where she will write pieces for specific charities to help fundraise for their cause. She is also in the process of writing her first poetry book.

Sam Berkson *p.12*
Sam Berkson is a poet, essayist and teacher. He has had two books published by Influx Press and runs the London branch of Hammer & Tongue, the UK's biggest network of slam poetry. A book of essays is due out with Influx Press in 2020 as well as a new book of poems with Active Press.

Benjamin Zephaniah *p.14*
Dr Benjamin Obadiah Iqbal Zephaniah was born and raised in Handsworth, Birmingham. At that time he called it the Jamaican capital of Europe due to the large Jamaican community there. His first real public performance was at 11 years old, and by the age of 15 he had attracted a strong following in Handsworth and had gained a reputation as a young poet who was capable of speaking on local and international issues. His poetry was strongly influenced by the music and poetry of Jamaica and what he called 'street politics'. At 22, he headed south to London where his first book *Pen Rhythm* was published. It was once said of him that he was the most filmed, most photographed, and most identifiable poet in Britain. His live performances on stage and, most of all, on television bought Dub Poetry straight into British living rooms. Benjamin's first book of children's poetry called *Talking Turkeys* went to the top of the children's book list straight after its publication. As well as writing poetry, novels, screenplays and stage plays, he has also written and presented documentaries for television and radio. He has been awarded 13 honorary doctorates in recognition of his work and a wing at The Ealing Hospital in West London has been named after him.

Tyra Mai *p.16*
As someone who identifies as an introvert, Tyra Mai uses poetry as a tool for introspection and self-reflection. Writing, hearing and reading poetry has enabled her to express her inner thoughts and feelings. For Tyra, poetry continues to be a major aid in dealing with social anxieties and other mental health obstacles and is something she believes can positively benefit everyone. Passionate about facilitating a space, where even more people can experience the positive effects poetry, Tyra founded POETclopedia.com; a poetry and spoken word platform focussed on creating a supportive and safe community for poets and other lyrical creatives to express themselves, share their work and engage and interact with other like-minded creatives. Find Tyra on Instagram @POETclopedia & @TyraMai.

Katie Dent *p.16*
Katie is 22 years old, born and raised in Canterbury, Kent, where she currently lives at home with her family and their many cats. Her love of all things book-related began when she was very small, and so naturally she has been attempting to write for almost as long. She recently graduated with a degree in English Literature from Oxford University, where she also published poems and articles in student anthologies. It was at university that she discovered the work of amazing contemporary poets like Warsan Shire and Saeed Jones, alongside older writers such as Elizabeth Bishop, Matthew Arnold and Andrew Marvell, all of whom are influences on her own work. Her experience of living abroad has given her a fascination with the themes of home and dislocation, and the wildly different feelings and responses that these things inspire, being produced not only by the place itself, but also by personality and circumstance.

Amalee Nsour *p.17*
Amalee Nsour is a Jordanian-American writer and poet. Her work appears in Jaffat El-Aqlam and Dardishi. Originally from the San Francisco Bay Area, she has lived in London for a few years, where she was able to witness and join the many dedicated efforts to make London a welcoming city for all - including with Unicef NEXT Gen and Akwaaba, a social center for asylum seekers. She now meanders between the US and Europe.

Salma El-Wardany *p.18*
Writer, poet and activist, Salma El-Wardany performs internationally, has given two TEDx Talks, worked with Edinburgh University on the Dangerous Woman project as well as partnering with The British Library, The Wellcome Collection and global brands. Being a Muslim woman of colour, she's struggled against stereotypes and marginalisation, specifically how difficult womanhood is in a patriarchal world. Her work centres around female storytelling and giving voice to the people history has for so long ignored. Salma lives in London where you can find her either running her marketing business, eating cake, performing poetry or writing about how the patriarchy is ruining all our lives. Failing that, find her on Instagram (@salmaelwardany) or Twitter (@writtenbysalma).

Camilla Thurlow *p.20*
Camilla Thurlow has worked globally as an explosive ordnance disposal specialist. She currently sits on the board of Indigo Volunteers.

Ruth Padel *p.21*
Ruth Padel's collection *The Mara Crossing* is a meditation on all aspects of migration. She's passionate about human rights and wildlife conservation (she has written a book on Asian tiger forests, a novel *Where the Serpent Lives*, featuring king cobras and ran writers' talks on endangered species at ZSL). Commissioned to write on Christmas, she researched homelessness in London for *Tidings, A Christmas Journey* (2016). Her next book *Beethoven Variations* (2020) is on the triumph of creativity over suffering. She is Professor of Poetry at King's College London and Fellow of the Royal Society of Literature. *Ripples on New Grass* was published in *The Mara Crossing: Poems on Migration* (Chatto & Windus 2012), reprinted by permission of Chatto & Windus.

Nikita Biswal *p.21*
Nikita Biswal loves to collect stories. She is a final year student of literature at King's College London and is currently writing about the idea of a city. She believes in breakfast, love and kindness. Her writing has previously been published by TLS, Strand, Network Capital and Forward Poetry.

Simone Yasmin *p.22*
Simone is a writer, born in the cultural mixing-pot of Leeds. Her love for poetry developed after she went to black-history poetry slam Rapoetry with her Dad in 2008. She experienced poetry performed by people like her, about people like her and for people like her. She felt inspired to tell her story and give voice to a narrative suppressed. Simone's blog *Ethereal Truth* reflects on issues of human-rights, race, gender and to quote her blog, *"things which the media overlooks and we, as functioning beings, unconsciously repress or ignore."* Simone's own experiences helped shape her work, though more recently she has worked to share the stories of those unable to voice their own. Her poetry emphasises her growth in working to take up all the space she needs, and Simone hopes her poetry teaches women to be just as unapologetic as she is learning to be. Website: etherealtruth.com. Instagram: @_etherealtruth.

Michelle Eghan *p.24*
Michelle started writing poetry when she was seven years old. She turned to writing to express feelings that she couldn't find a way to say. Poetry helped Michelle deal with situations that she couldn't talk about and now she shares her writing in hopes it will help others.

Taj Babiker *p.25*
Taj (or Tag) was born in Sudan and has been in the UK as a refugee for about six months. Taj loved everything in his country. Now, he is studying ESOL, maths and IT, is in the Cadets and plays football and athletics. He volunteers with Friends of Refugees which he sees as a family. In winter, he wants to help with distributing clothes and food to refugees. In the UK he likes the people as he thinks they're very helpful. He would like to do IT in the future and work at Microsoft – that is his dream.

Bec Thompson aka Versailles *p.25*
26-year-old Sydney sider Versailles writes candidly about her struggles with mental illness and addiction. Using Instagram as a creative outlet, @Versaillessings shares the emotional ups and downs of journey in recovery from addiction, PTSD and BPD to obliterate the stigma and ignorance that surrounds mental illness. She encourages an open dialect around mental health, it's importance in our lives and how both the individual and society may better manage mental illness.

Fisky *p.26*
Fisky is a poet, rapper, public speaker and Founder of Mind Over Matter (MoM), a monthly event where mental health is discussed through spoken word, Hip Hop and song. Fisky started @mindovermatterldn the day he got sober after a twenty-year battle with depression and addiction. Since then, Fisky has watched it become the platform he never had. The event has helped people with depression, addiction, anxiety and opening difficult conversations. MoM has collaborated with TEDx, The Lost Lectures, The Tavistock & Portman and recently hosted their first international event in Melbourne, Australia. Fisky is recording his second album *Cheaper Than Therapy* due for release in late 2019. His work has been featured on BBC Radio 6, BBC Radio London, Fubar Radio, ITCH FM and many more. He has delivered speeches at The London Academy of Excellence and ITV. Writing has always been Fisky's therapist. He draws on his twenty years lived experience with depression and addiction to raise awareness, let people know they aren't alone, process his own struggles and project positive energy. Fisky is also part of the #FLOpoet collective mentored by Natalie 'Floacist' Stewart, founding member of Multi Grammy nominated Neo Soul group, Floetry.

Esi Yankey aka Miss Yankey *p.28*
A British/Ghanaian writer and performance poet, Miss Yankey captivates people with her honest and heartfelt poetry which she often uses to advocate for the oppressed and silenced. An International Slam Champion, co-host and resident poet at The Chocolate Poetry Club, open mic host at Mind Over Matter, and member of London's unrivalled FLO Poets. The Autumn of 2019 sees the release of her much-anticipated book *More Than a Machine* from which her poem *The Oracles Oath* is taken. *More Than a Machine* is an honest account of one woman's experience with mental illness. The poems in her candid collection express pain through relatable poetry - from dealing with anxiety, depression and PTSD, to sharing the heartbreak of losing loved ones to mental illness. Bookings and enquiries: info@missyankey.com Instagram, Twitter and YouTube: @MissYankey. Facebook: /checkmissyankey.

Kashif Khan *p.31*
Kashif Khan is a 23-year-old refugee from Pakistan. In November 2015, whilst studying computer science at university, the Taliban attempted to recruit Kashif for his computer skills. Kashif refused. The Taliban then beheaded his cousin after arresting him for not disclosing where Kashif was. He fled for not only his safety, but his family's. Kashif walked from Pakistan to Iran, through Turkey to Bulgaria. During this time, Kashif was once without food for three days, and begun eating bark. In Bulgaria, Kashif says he experienced torture at the hands of the police, stating dogs tore our clothes and flesh. After being released, he moved through Croatia, Slovakia, Austria, Germany and Italy. He now lives in Paris, where his most painful moment yet was finding out his grandmother in Pakistan had died, and he couldn't go to her funeral. *"As refugees, we are usually treated like animals. We are humans, we have the same blood and we are living on the same earth."*

Ramla Ali p.32

Ramla Ali is the Somali war refugee who – until last year – hid her entire boxing career from her family. She is a two time UK national champion and the African Zonal Champion. In 2018, alongside her husband-and-coach Richard Moore, Ali helped create the Somali boxing federation from the UK, with the intention of Ali representing Somalia at world level and competing in the AIBA Women's World Boxing Championship. As a young, Muslim woman involved with boxing, Ali strongly believes that it is her responsibility to educate her community on the importance of women participating in sport.

Karrim Jalalli p.33

Karrim Jalali writes poetry, essays, plays and fiction and works in local government. In addition to writing in his spare time, he also campaigns on environmental issues for Fossil Free Southwark.

Quinton Green aka Mr Milise p.34

Northampton born Quinton Green aka Mr Milise has been plying his trade as a lyricist for more than 15 Years and credits Mike Skinner from The Streets for his exposure to the world of spoken word. As a youngster Milise would experiment with poetry and the art of storytelling on a beat as well as creating thought provoking acapellas. His work and performances have been positively received and some of his pieces have been used by police forces, schools, youth clubs and councils as part of youth awareness initiatives across the UK. His intention is to adopt a role as a voice for the voiceless and hopes to grow a platform/network on the poetry circuit to help communicate a message from those who have faced challenging circumstances and adversity. Follow Mr Milise's Journey @whoismrmilise.

Anna McNutt p.36

Anna McNutt is an award-winning writer and filmmaker based in London. Half American and half Serbian-Slovene, Anna embraces multiculturalism and cosmopolitism. Yet, the subject of 'home' continues to be a difficult one and she remains critical of the current global political climate, particularly interested in the clash between Eastern and Western values. Her poem, titled, *Well, I'm not nice at all* pertains to the painful memories that continue to linger on in the Balkans post the break-up of Yugoslavia. Anna's poetry often explores the fragmentation and construction of identity, contrasting dream-like fantasizes with harsh and uncomfortable truths. Anna is a recent graduate with an MA in Filmmaking (Producing) and BA in Media & Communications, specializing in Creative Writing & Journalism, from Goldsmiths, University of London. To read more of her work, go to: https://annamcnutt.com.

Dizraeli p.37

Poet, singer, MC and multi-instrumentalist Dizraeli is a genre all of his own and is long established as a gem of the spoken word world. In the past few years, having won the BBC Poetry Slam Championship and led the ground-breaking band Dizraeli & The Small Gods to underground success, Dizraeli has built himself a cult following around Europe and played to audiences of thousands around the world. Now, after two years working with refugees in Calais, studying percussion in Senegal, and immersing himself in the world of London grime and bass music, he's back with *The Unmaster*, his first self-produced album and an electrifying new sound, the first single from which has already won support from BBC 6 Music and Gilles Peterson's Worldwide FM.

Danny Collins p.38

After almost five years of homelessness, Danny spends his time writing poetry, tour guiding with the Invisible Cities (Manchester), volunteering and raising awareness. At 17, he joined the army as a way of escaping a three-year prison sentence for fighting in the street (after he was deeply affected by his father's death). Proving wrong the cynics who told him he wouldn't last a week, he was discharged after 13 years. Danny struggled to adapt to civilian life after service and spent a lot of time away from his wife and daughters due to construction work. He was then seriously injured at work. His mental health deteriorated as he struggled with the inability to work. Depression and heavy drinking followed. Danny found support at Manchester's Booth Centre, Walking With The Wounded and the Veteran's Association. It was during this period he was diagnosed with PTSD. In 2019, Danny's collection of poetry was published in his first book called *Off the Cobbles* – it is a deeply-moving firsthand account of homelessness in modern Britain. His poems of love, loss and acceptance reconnect us with what it means to be human: to fall, fail and recover.

Inua Ellams p.39
Born in Nigeria, Inua Ellams is a poet, playwright and performer, graphic artist and designer. He is a Complete Works poet alumni and a graphic designer at White Space Creative Agency. He facilitates workshops in creative writing where he explores reoccurring themes in his work - identity, displacement and destiny - in accessible, enjoyable ways for participants of all ages and backgrounds. His creative work has been recognised with a number of awards: the Live Canon International Poetry Prize, the Arts Council of England Award, a Wellcome Trust Award, twice shortlisted for the Brunel Prize for African Poetry, longlisted the Alfred Fagan Award, Edinburgh Fringe First Award 2009 and the Liberty Human Rights Award. He has been commissioned by the Royal Shakespeare Company, National Theatre, Tate Modern, Louis Vuitton, Chris Ofili, BBC Radio and Television. His first three pamphlets of poetry *Thirteen Fairy Negro Tales* and *Candy Coated Unicorn and Converse* were published Flipped Eye and *The Wire-Headed Heathen* by Akashic Books. Several plays including the critically acclaimed *Black T-shirt Collection* and award-winning *The 14th Tale* are published by Oberon. In 2005, he founded the Midnight Run— an arts-filled, night-time, playful, walking, urban movement that attempts to reconnect inner city lives with inner-city spaces.

Muzoon Almellehan p.40
Muzoon Almellehan, 21, is a Syrian refugee and education activist and the first refugee to be named a UNICEF Goodwill Ambassador. Muzoon has been campaigning for children's education in emergencies since she was forced to flee Syria in 2013 with her family. Muzoon offers a powerful authentic voice on education in emergencies. She is also a No Lost Generation (NLG) campaign champion for UNICEF Middle East and North Africa. She has spoken to world leaders at high-level events including the UN General Assembly, and the G20, and has visited Chad, Jordan and Mali with UNICEF. Muzoon is the recipient of many awards including BBC's list of 100 influential and inspirational women, TIME's 30 Most Influential Teens, Teen Vogue's 21 Under 21 and Glamour Woman of the Year Award. She is currently studying at University in the United Kingdom.

Sophie Haydock p.42
Sophie Haydock is a journalist (Sunday Times, Guardian, BBC Three), editor and winner of the 2018 Impress Prize for New Writers, for her novel about the women who inspired the Austrian artist Egon Schiele. She is also associate director of the Word Factory, an organisation dedicated to short stories. Twitter: @SophieHaydock.

Nida Elley p.44
Nida Elley is a teacher, writer, and editor who has lived in Lahore, New York, Austin, and now London. She recently began a blog, *Lovelorn* (http://lovelorn.me), to write about the disconnectedness so many of us feel with the world around us. Her fiction was published by Bloomsbury UK in a Pakistani-themed, Jane Austen-inspired anthology, *Austenistan* (2018).

Mikala Monsoon aka Kardashoon p.48
Mikala is a 23-year-old creative from Glasgow. She has her fingers in multiple arty pies, including makeup, creative direction, writing and sketching. Mikala is super passionate about feminism and sex-positivity, including working to remove the stigma surrounding sex work. She likes to incorporate these subjects into her art as much as possible, as she believes art in any form is the easiest way to communicate and digest. Mikala also tries her best to speak on mental health, as well as addiction. *"I believe these subjects are intrinsically linked and after struggling with addiction myself, I'd like to see current ideas of why it happens to be shifted, in particular starting by removing blame from those affected, and treating it as the disease it truly is."* Only with the removal of damaging stigmas surrounding supposedly 'taboo' subjects can we truly move forward as a society. Socials @kardashoon and website: www.mixmua.com.

Hayah Khan p.49
Hayah is a South Londoner with a mixed English and Pakistani heritage. Her writing journey began in January 2019 and she started performing her pieces in April 2019. She writes to heal herself and others, exploring empowerment, freedom and raising awareness on issues such as homelessness and social issues that we face. Through words, Hayah connects to strangers, spreading kindness and positivity. She hopes to inspire and unite people, as love is always her message.

Dipal Acharya p.49
Dipal Acharya is a London-based journalist and editor. Having worked in the industry for over 10 years, she is a proud first generation British Asian writer that specialises in arts and culture coverage. She is presently the Arts and Entertainment Director at ES Magazine (London Evening Standard). She has also contributed to the Daily Telegraph, the Observer Magazine and Dazed & Confused, among other titles. Travel is one of her greatest passions and remains a rich source of inspiration for her work in helping to improve diversity and representation in journalism both in the UK and abroad. She lives in north London with her husband Maanas, a barrister, and their daughter Mila.

Kai-Isaiah Jamal p.50
Kai-Isaiah Jamal is a spoken word poet, performer, writer, model and trans visibility activist. He works alongside institutions and brands to bring a voice to the misrepresented or unrepresented QTIPOC. Working with Dazed, Vice, ID, Stella McCartney, Tate and with his own family collective BBZ, he aims to prioritise the voice and safety of queer people of colour. His work disrupts the cis-het normality as well as aims to diversify the literature sphere with young, working class, queer and trans magic that he wishes he could have had access to growing up. Find him on Instagram @kai_isaiah_jamal.

Anthony Ramsay aka Anthony No Filter p.54
Anthony was born on April fools but he's far from a joke! He is a black British, Caribbean boy from East London. He is vulgar, sensual, sensitive and honest when he becomes Anthony No Filter - who dares to say the things that he would only say around the comfort of his friends. Anthony attended a local stage school from the age 10 through to 14. The sass, the drama and the confidence comes from there. Stopping is his biggest regret. Spoken word and poetry is his re-entry into performing. *"I was knocked by my insecurities and an identity crisis at 17. I battled with my sexuality, not fitting and struggling to answer those questions which I HATE so much; 'What do you want to do?', 'Who do you want to be?'"* Now at 24, he lives, laughs and loves without a script. It's in the name... @Anthonynofilter!

Ingrid Marsh aka the Badass Gal p.57
Ingrid Marsh is a motivational speaker, confidence expert, growth mindset trainer, and NLP Practitioner. On a mission to shatter the inextricable link between gender/race and ability, at age 50 (and looking nothing like the stereotypical park runner) she vlogged her transformation from a couch potato to a runner in the park by running every day for 30-days in the rain and killer snow the media dubbed, The Beast From The East.

Sophie Leseberg Smith aka The Nasty Poet p.60
South London poet, Sophie aka The Nasty Poet, is the author of the *Nasty The Audiobook*, produced by Grime's Blay Vision. Her performances include the ICA, Boiler Room, Keep Hush, Earth Hackney and Just Jam to name a few. She has written commission work for a wide variety of purposes, from exhibitions to commercials to circus arts shows and has been featured across Nowness, Vogue and Clash Magazine.

Tash Monterisi aka T.MONTERISI p.62
T.MONTERISI, is a writer and painter living in Leeds. Exploring the human condition through provocative spoken word pieces, themes of honesty and accountability run heavily through T.MONTERISI's work. Performing on various stages from London to Edinburgh, her poetry is raw and evokes a change of perspective, one belly at a time.

Othman A Kareem p.65
Othman is an Iraqi refugee who has been living in the UK for four years, but he continues to like the Iraqi culture and misses it. He likes the people in the UK – *"when you're stuck or you don't know what you're doing, someone will help you."* He's studying BTEC Business and in the future, he'd like to develop his own business. He enjoys spending his time at the gym, hanging out with friends and eating out at restaurants. He cares about his education, which he regards as the most important thing to him.

Catrin Nye p.66
Catrin Nye is a television journalist who has reported all over the world for the BBC. She is part of the steering committee for Unicef's Next Generation London.

Conscious Rhymes *p.70*

Conscious Rhymes is a poet, spoken word artist, podcaster and provoker of thought. His mission is to revolutionize through the medium of word, by tackling pressing, relevant and topical societal, political and personal issues. He wants to challenge himself and others creatively and think on a deeper level about all of the problems we face as humans, and the toxic ideologies which act as foundations for them. Conscious Rhymes is London born and bred, currently studying for a degree in Civil Engineering. More examples of his work, podcasts and projects he's working on can be found on his Instagram @ConsciousRhymes_. *"I owe any and all success I've been granted to The Most High, and I pray I can continue to work for justice and truth on this earth."*

Khalil Aldabbas *p.72*

Khalil is a refugee from Damascus in Syria. He has been in the UK for five years and is going university to become an engineer. *"I wish to all refugees to have a safe life, full of happiness and success. Let's care about each others and rebuild what is destroyed."*

Sophie Shepherd *p.73*

Sophie Shepherd is a 22-year-old just finishing her MA in Poetic Practice at Royal Holloway. Sophie writes poems and loves to perform all over London at various open mics and poetry nights as much as she can, whilst trying to be wary of her student budget.

Riaz Phillips *p.74*

Riaz Phillips is a writer, born and based in London. His first independently published book *Belly Full: Caribbean Food in the UK*, via Tezeta Press was inspired by his own Jamaican upbringing and became an award winning endeavour sold in shops, bookstores, and galleries across the world.

Tannika Williams-Nelson *p.75*

Tannika is a London based fashion designer, four times published author and spoken word artist. Writing has always been a passion of hers since publishing her first book at the age of 15. Her published work includes fiction, non-fiction and poetry. Poetry is a way for her to express her thoughts and feelings subliminally, and fashion allows her to express her personality through crochet. For books/poetry www.timeismoneymedia.com and for fashion www.uniqueboutiquelondon.co.uk.

Hiba Jahangir *p.76*

Hiba is a 17-year-old based in North West London. As a young Muslim Pakistani female who is an advocate for human rights, she thinks it is crucial for change to be made in this world, especially with the level of injustices and human rights abuses seen in today's society. She hopes to do this through educating people at spoken word nights. Hiba also believes that actions speak louder than words, and therefore she began volunteering which allowed her see how a small act of kindness can have a huge impact. *'O you who believe! Stand out firmly for justice, as witnesses to Allah, even if it be against yourselves, your parents, and your relatives, or whether it is against the rich or the poor...'* (Quran 4:135). Find her on Instagram @hiba.ax.

Samira Seini aka SamiRhymes *p.77*

Samira/SamiRhymes is a London based spoken word poet and voiceover artist. Samira started her writing journey young and had poems published at the ages of nine, 10 and 11. Topics included the Millenium Dome, boys and the world. At the age of 13 Samira's approach become more spoken. She developed a love for rhyming and from this derived her poetical name SamiRhymes. Samira writes, raps and speaks about various topics in her journey of life. This includes her journey to God after embracing Islam, growing up, positive and negative experiences, family, relationships and identity. SamiRhymes has performed at a number of venues including Goldsmiths and Kingston University, cafes, restaurants and at other private events. In 2011 SamiRhymes produced a rhyming voiceover narrative for a charity's TV advert. In July 2019, Samira won her first Poetry Slam competition; Word4Word.

Georgia Eigbe *p.83*

Georgia Eigbe lives in South East London. *"Fun fact about me: I am blasian, my mother is from Sri Lanka and my father is from Nigeria."* Her faith is the contributing factor behind her writing, as she is a born again Christian. She gave her life to the Lord in 2017, and through growing in her relationship with God, she has been able to use her poetry to glorify Him and His wonderful works. As a shy person who struggles to talk to people, she uses poetry as expression, following her new-found confidence through her faith. *"I write to bring freedom and peace to the world!"* Instagram @Georgiaaa_writes.

Dan Considine aka Acafella *p.78*
Acafella is a poet from North London who holds a passion for vivid storytelling and human observation. Refusing to be tied down to any style or theme, he is versatile in his topic of poem and known for his energetic performances that begin with *"I'm going to poem the shit out of you."* Acafella discovered the incredible healing power of poemin' after a long cycle of substance misuse and battles with poor mental health that culminated in two traumatic events occurring within a few weeks of each other. He uses his excessive and relentless energy to share his own story and desires for a kinder world with as many people as he can. He's gonna poem the shit out of you... Twitter/ Instagram: @_acafella.

Danny Martin *p.80*
@dannymartin29 is a London based spoken word performer and story teller who aims to share people's truths through stories. The world around us is evolving so quickly that we're forgetting the importance of humanity and that we all go through different things. Therefore, through his pieces, Danny aims to resonate with the 'everyman's' issues and lifestyles.

Marlon Roudette *p.81*
Marlon Roudette is a British/Vincentian songwriter and recording artist. Originally from Harrow Road, West London, he moved with his mother to St. Vincent and the Grenadines in the Caribbean at the age of eight. Since moving back to London, aged 18, he has gone on to become a multi-platinum artist in his own right but also as a songwriter for artists such as Mabel and Not3s. In 2014 he was officially recognised as a Cultural Ambassador to St. Vincent and the Grenadines and has continued his work to promote Caribbean talent on both sides of the pond.

Mequannt Assefa *p.82*
Mequannt was born and raised in Ethiopia and came to the UK two years ago. He has refugee status and is happy to be living a free life in the UK (but misses the food of home). He is currently studying ESOL at Southgate College. He is passionate about writing his own music to explore all the different aspects of his life. In the future, he also wants to use his artistic talent in the theatre as an actor, director, and writer. He is passionate about helping other people and wants to see better

support for refugees and asylum seekers so that none end up homeless. His poem in Amharic is about being deeply in love, with powerful lines translating to *"my heart has been so disturbed since I saw you."*

Ahmed Noori *p.84*
Ahmed Noori is a refugee from Kabul, Afghanistan. He has lived in the UK for over three years. Currently he's studying A-levels and cannot wait to go to university as his aspiration is to become a politician (to bring about positive changes in society and create a platform to improve people's lives). He would like to alter people's negative perceptions about refugees and immigrants; help them to recognise both sides of the story, not only the cynical stereotypes. Ahmed loves the UK as he feels it's a great country for individuals to prosper, if we facilitate them to receive the right support, at the right time. This undoubtedly will prompt a civic culture of giving back to community. Those who receive support today will certainly assist those who need support tomorrow.

Billy Lockett *p.84*
Billy Lockett is a British singer-songwriter from Northampton, best known for his infectious pop ballads including *Every Time You're High*. Billy started playing the piano at age eight and has had no lessons. He started a band at age 15 and continued playing in a dingy little pub. He cites Radiohead and Italian composer Ludovico Einaudi as influences. By 2014, Lockett was earning a name for himself, supporting Lana Del Ray, Birdy and KT Tunstall. It was during this time that his father passed away. For the next two years, Lockett wrote songs in the basement with only his piano and his producer Phil Clark for company. Lockett released his debut EP *Burn It Down* in 2016, which was championed by BBC Introducing and went on to amass an impressive 1.6 million streams on Spotify. In 2017, he released a live EP. His debut album will be released late 2019.

Sophie Hardcastle *p.85*
Sophie Hardcastle is an author, poet and visual artist from Sydney, Australia. She works as a research assistant in the English Faculty at the University of Oxford. In 2018, she was a Provost's Scholar in English Literature at the University of Oxford. She graduated from the University of Sydney with First Class Honours in Visual Arts in 2017, receiving the University

of Sydney's Academic Merit Award. Sophie is the author of *Running Like China* (Hachette, 2015), and *Breathing Under Water* (Hachette, 2016). Her books have been longlisted for national book awards in Australia and made lists such as Dymock's Best Books for 2016. Allen & Unwin will publish her first novel for adults, *Below Deck*, in 2020. Sophie is also the co-creator, co-writer and co-director of the Australian miniseries *Cloudy River*, which is produced by unko, and currently in post-production with The Editors. Sophie has travelled to Antarctica, Patagonia, France and Switzerland for artist residencies. In 2018, she was the winner of the University of Oxford's Rebecca West Essay Prize, and has also written for publications such as ELLE, Harper's Bazaar, The Anthroposphere and The Stick. Her art has been published in Industry Magazine, RISE Journal and The Mays Anthology. As a mental health spokesperson, Sophie has also spoken to over 15,000 young people across Australia, appeared on national radio programs, and in 2017, was made a World Mental Health Ambassador.

Travis De Vries *p.86*
Travis De Vries is a Gamilaroi conceptual artist based in the Hunter Valley region of Australia. Travis creates everything from large scale experiential art works to intimate storytelling moments, making contemporary fables that draw on his rich Aboriginal Gamilaroi heritage yet deal with a range of themes from the highly political and global to the extremely personal and emotional. Travis also co-hosts the comedy podcast *Broriginals*.

Joelle Taylor *p.88*
Joelle Taylor is an award-winning poet, playwright and author who has recently completed touring Europe, Australia and South East Asia with her latest collection *Songs My Enemy Taught Me*. She is widely anthologised, the author of three full poetry collections and three plays and is currently completing her debut book of short stories *The Night Alphabet*, with support from the Arts Council. She has featured on *The Verb* (R3), *Power Lines* (R4), *Poetry Please* (Radio 4), *Educating the East End* (ITV), and *We Belong Here* (BBC). Joelle founded SLAMbassadors, the UK's national youth slam championships, for the Poetry Society in 2001 and was its Artistic Director and National Coach until 2018. Her work is taught as part of the OCR GCSE syllabus, and she

has received a Change Maker Award from the Southbank Centre in recognition of the effect SLAMbassadors had on British culture. She has recently been commissioned to develop a new spoken word show to tour throughout 2019/2020 and is the Founder and Artistic Director of a new inter-European spoken word project *Borderlines*, funded by the Arts Council. She is the host and co-curator of premier London poetry and music club Out-Spoken, and a Fellow of the RSA. She was longlisted for the Jerwood Compton Poetry Fellowship 2018. © Joelle Taylor.

Leanne Shorley *p.90*
Leanne Shorley is an actor, writer and spoken word poet living in Lambeth. She regularly performs in poetry, cabaret and comedy nights across London. Described as *"the lovechild of Jo Brand and Pam Ayres,"* her style of irreverent observations tap in to the beauty and absurdity of everyday life. Taking serious questions about love, and putting them through her female, millennial gaze, she explores relationships with irony and humour in the hope that people will find solace in her words and imagery. *Ear* explores dependency in relationships and celebrates the unsung friends and family who allow us to be free.

Wendy Mackenzie *p.92*
Born in Yorkshire, Wendy lived her early life in a caravan, working the land and rearing animals. From her early dreams of being a butcher she instead became a beautician. Emigrating to Australia in her early-twenties, following the man she then loved, they gave birth to her daughter Sophie, Co-Founder of Words By, and a son named Danny. After 25 years together, her husband took a new path. Suffering from heartbreak and depression, she has slowly recovered for the past five years and has now found strength in a love for all things spontaneous. Wendy values kindness above all else and is thankful for the grace and humility that she always allows herself to have.

Natasha Badrov *p.92*
Natasha is a typical Piscean - compassionate, intuitive, pleasure seeking, imaginative, dramatic and thrives off the energy of others. She grew up in beautiful Sydney and spent a few years in her beloved London Town where she fell in love with travel, foreign cities and enchanting men and women. Natasha has kept a journal since she was five

years old. With the encouragement of her mother to write her feelings out, instead of bottling them up inside, she turned to words for expression and comfort. Through bouts of anxiety and depression she has been able to find a release in her writing. Natasha struggles with her own feelings of loneliness and never wants others to feel the same way so she writes her romantic notions, deepest fantasies and late-night feelings as a way of relating to others on a soul level. Instagram: @natasha_katarina.

Mr Gee p.93
Mr Gee has been a veteran of the UK poetry scene for 20 years. Perhaps best known as the *"Poet Laureate"* on Russell Brand's Radio 2 show, he's also presented the series *Poetic Justice* on Radio 4 detailing his rehabilitative work in prisons. *"Charming and politically articulate"* –The Times. © Mr Gee.

basq-Lyon p.94
@basqlyon has loved writing for his whole life, but admits it was limited to the back of his priorities. It wasn't until around 17 when he lost all sense of self that he reached out for the pen. *"I let my soul cry through poetry. I told the page all of the pain I felt."* Looking back, he now sees that this was the beginning of a journey to healing and self-understanding. *"I believe it's my responsibility to share this journey with anyone who may cross my path."*

Joel Baker p.97
Joel Baker, the Nottingham native, is a Radio 1 play-listed artist, drawing inspirations from Bob Dylan and J Dilla. His music was put into the spotlight after being discovered when Taylor Swift found his music on Spotify. A former Parliamentary speech writer, Joel left the House Of Commons to pursue music and has been touring around Europe and America. His recent song with chart topper Mahalia is called *Catch Me When I Fall* and is available on all streaming platforms.

Sade Hewitt-Ibru p.98
Sade Hewitt-Ibru MA, 50-plus, is British of Jamaican heritage currently residing in the UK. Her personal journeys of struggle are not easily forgotten but she has learnt to forgive. Her resoluteness has developed compassion for others and renewed her character along the way. She has found that words of love can sometimes be empty whereas the demonstration of love can be life changing. Sade has been participating in a two-year theatre project with Public Acts, Shakespeare's *Pericles*, National Theatre, and *As You Like It*, Queen's Theatre. The company of community group participants, professional actors and theatre staff, has been to her an amazing example of how extremely diverse communities can work together peacefully, respecting each other. She has previously written to support charity funding for Open Age. Some of her personal life experiences, the need for prayer and hope in her life, inspired this poem.

Ezra Porter p.100
Ezra Porter is a 21-year-old from South London. She shares her ideas and life experiences through creative writing. Ezra's personal struggles have been receiving judgment from others but *"with my confidence I have grown to remain confident within who I am."* In the future she hopes and aims to create movies to expand her creativeness in visual form.

Legacy Russell p.102
Legacy Russell is a curator, writer, and artist. Born and raised in New York City, her work focuses on gender, performance, digital selfdom, Internet idolatry and new media ritual.

Azareen Van der Vliet Oloomi p.108
Azareen Van der Vliet Oloomi is the author of the novels *Call Me Zebra* and *Fra Keeler*. She has won a Whiting Writers' Award and a National Book Foundation 5 Under 35 award, and is the recipient of a Fulbright Fellowship, a fellowship from the Institució de les Lletres Catalanes in Barcelona, and residency fellowships from the MacDowell Colony and Ledig House. She has lived in Iran, Spain, Italy, the United Arab Emirates, and currently teaches in the M.F.A. Program in Creative Writing at the University of Notre Dame, splitting her time between South Bend, Indiana and Florence, Italy.

Joanna Jarvis p.110
Joanna began volunteering with Care4Calais in the winter of 2015, before The Jungle was destroyed. She volunteered at Jungle Books teaching English. Often those she taught shared their harrowing stories of why and how they were forced to flee their homes and make the dangerous journeys to Calais - she hopes that her poem gives a voice to those she met in The Jungle.

Briona Lamback *p.111*
Briona Lamback is a poet and traveller, inspired by the places she visits and most importantly, by the human connections made along the way. Briona is passionate about helping more people of color see the world and making people feel something with her words.

Vanessa Aida *p.112*
Vanessa Aida is a lover of words, whether that be expressed through poetry, music, books or films. What began as a therapeutic practice of journaling, soon evolved into poetry, where she created an Instagram page to share her work, as well as performing at spoken word events. *"Words hold so much power and this is one of the reasons which prompted me to begin writing."* Born and raised in South London in an underprivileged area, Vanessa is passionate about seeing people thrive, regardless of their background. This led her to previously volunteer with a homeless charity. Additionally, Vanessa has a keen interest in personal development and hopes to encourage and inspire others with her writing. Find her on Instagram @vanessaaida_writes.

Luke Smith *p.114*
Luke Smith (@ls_wordy) is a self-published poet and author of his 2018 chapbook, *A Reflective State* and eagerly anticipated, 2019 Poetry Collective, *these things i see*. Luke began writing to combat episodes of Post-Traumatic Stress Disorder (PTSD) following military service and operational combat duty overseas in the Former Republic of Yugoslavia and Iraq. Luke's craft sees him write personal pieces about his childhood, anxiety and the intrinsic fear of loss. Poetry has become an ink-elixir to his own (unique) personal struggles in love and life. A proud father, Luke enjoys music, film, tennis and cooking.

Ruby Bayley-Pratt *p.114*
Ruby grew up in Ecuador until aged nine, when her family decided to move back to the UK... the Highlands of Scotland of all places. Ever since, she's spent her life trying to reconcile the impact of this upheaval and the cultures of these places on her identity; never quite belonging anywhere. She tries to keep Latin America alive in her heart through music, language, food, and the occasional trip back, whilst also continuing to learn about her privilege in this context. She has been committed to contributing to social change in her community and the world from a young age; from fundraising to saving her local village hall as a teenager and working in the relief effort of the Great Fire of Valparaíso as a student, to campaigning to end sexual harassment in the charity sector and volunteering as a trustee. She is a fundamental believer in the art of protest. Her motivator is anger. She can be found on Twitter and Instagram @RubyBayleyPratt.

Sharmay Mitchell *p.115*
Sharmay is a softly-spoken, avidly-writing, poetry-loving, cat-appreciating, voracious creator. Her April 2017 personal commitment to produce one creative piece each day, has so far carried her to over 900 consecutive days of all things artsy (visual and literature) which she shares on her Instagram page @758.767.

Aarushi Agrawal *p.116*
Aarushi is a writer and editor who strongly believes in the power of words to open minds and communicate ideas.

Katy Lagden *p.144*
Katy Lagden is a freelance writer and poet based in the UK. Her work has appeared in various online and print publications. She has a particular interest in writing for platforms and organisations that aim to help others, normalise taboos and open up conversations on important issues.

Fran Lock *p.117*
Fran Lock is a sometime-itinerant dog whisperer, and author of five poetry collections, most recently *Dogtooth* (Out Spoken Press, 2017), and *Ruses and Fuses* (Culture Matters, 2018) in collaboration with collage artist Steev Burgess. Her next collection, *Contains Mild Peril*, is due to be published by Out Spoken Press late 2019. Fran is a post-doctoral candidate in her final year of a practice-based PhD at Birkbeck University.

Simon Maddrell *p.118*
Simon Maddrell was born in Douglas, Isle of Man in 1965 and brought up in Bolton, Lancashire. He has lived in London since 1999. Simon spent 15 years in the corporate sector. In 2002, he founded and ran award-winning charity Excellent Development for another 15 years. Driven by his Queer Manx identity, Simon has sought to seek the truth in the finest words he can find since 2012. Simon regularly performs spoken word in London.

Conor McCarthy p.120
Conor McCarthy is a charity fundraiser, volunteer, blogger and writer. His academic background in sociology has lent him a broad understanding of many topics. His main focus at university was to explore the motivations of refugee volunteers. Being from Hackney, London, Conor was lucky enough to live in a highly multicultural community. From a young age he has also explored the world and its cultures, hoping to gain a greater understanding of the nuanced and fragile world that we live in. As well as recently starting a website at worldrocksteady. blog, he has written several articles for The Mancunion newspaper.

Memo Brown p.123
Memo Brown is a poet, spoken word artist and bookworm from Brixton, South East London. Writing is her side hobby which she uses as a form of catharsis for how she feels and sees the world around her. You can find her @b.memo.brown on Instagram where she remains semi anonymous due to her day job and posts various forms of poetry for anyone to enjoy or relate to. Her love of reading is currently inspiring her to write her own book which she hopes to publish and present in the not too distant future!

Abdullah Mohammed p.123
Abdullah is a refugee from Afghanistan. He is studying A-levels in History, Politics and Economics at Sixth Form College. He likes the United Kingdom's role in world globalisation, the rule of law and democracy. He loves boxing, and cares about human freedom, equality, global law and order and finally, peace and stability. He'd like to see change for migrant young people by having access to better and higher education. Afghans are proud of their identity culture, and therefore, they respect others identity and culture. He is proud of his history which gives him a sense of responsibility and having an optimistic vision for the future makes him who he is.

Rebecca Kunijwok-Kwawang aka Becksy Becks p.124
Becksy Becks is a Flopoet, a lover of words and an appreciator of sounds. Everything she does in life is centred around her three main pillars; laughter, love and literature. She describes herself as *"a poet by passion, dancer by daydream and awesome by everything else."*

Tinoula Ibrahim p.126
A creative at heart, Tinoula is studying at the University of Warwick and balancing her love of the arts. *"I am a woman moulded by the plethora of poems, novels and scripts memorised throughout my childhood."* Understanding the potent power of words, she chooses to use hers to make a difference and project her voice to reveal and channel inner emotions. Raised in London under a Nigerian household, Tinoula is well acquainted with the importance of cultures and heritage. She was chosen to write the script for a production celebrating Afro-Caribbean culture at her university and has used the opportunity to educate and inspire her audience about both culture and today's society. *"I like to believe I am a young woman with a unique vision, integrity and a promising future, hoping to one day fulfil my dream of being within the creative industry whilst also pursuing my law degree."*

Joseph Lee p.128
Joseph has been creating caustic yet compassionate poetic prose for the past five years, sharing spoken word when his word is intended to be heard. Acknowledging his ongoing internal tussle between nurture and nature, Joseph's work explores ideas of family structure, intimate relationships, loss, isolation, environment and fulfilment. His work continues to parade in the middle ground of colloquial working class angst and existential acceptance.

Mahwash Chaudary p.129
Mahwash has always been mesmerised by words. Starting to write at a young age she used her words as a way of making sense of the world around her, often taking solace and finding peace in putting pen to paper. She prides herself on unlearning many cultural and societal behaviours that often lead her to feel isolated, closed off and 'other'. She has now embraced her 'otherness' and instead uses it as a vice to propel her creative works. Mahwash's poem Medusa seeks to give some insight into how turbulent pasts can manifest in people's personas and the impact of trauma in shaping one's identity. She is currently working on two features. The *Trifecta* is a three-part collection, *Hive* (family and society), *Heart* (relationships) and *Homecoming* (identity and self awareness). The second feature is a collection of writings in a series called *Letters To My Children* which is a personal exploration of the internal dialogue of parenthood.

Andrew Franks *p.134*
Andrew Franks was born in Eastbourne, England in the early 1960's. He has worked in local government, theatre, as an English language teacher, a cycle courier in London, a musician and for magazine and newspaper companies around the world. He currently lives on Sydney's Northern Beaches and he performs his poetry on a regular basis in both Sydney and London. In addition, he hosts a weekly radio show *London Calling* on Sydney's 2RRR and plays guitar in two bands, The fReds and The Butterfly House. His first collection *Scratched in the stars, sprawled on the sand* (Soul Bay, 2009), has had to be reprinted four times. His second collection, *The last of the great British traitors* (Soul Bay, 2011), was in part inspired by his father's autobiography (discovered posthumously). Franks also contributed *Engels' Ashes* to a short story compilation *Thirteen* (Soul Bay, 2013). His third collection of poetry, *Sunflower Eclipse over Troia Nova* (Soul Bay, 2018), was published in November 2018. *Sunflower Casanova*, a film of his live poetry has been shown as part of the Sydney Independent film festival. © Soul Bay Press 2019.

Jasmine 'MeiMei' Stephens *p.136*
Jasmine, 18, grew up around East London and had the privilege of traveling around the world from a young age, influencing the way she lives her life and how she constructs perceptions. Growing up mixed, Swedish and Chinese, made her cherish her heritage and learn to love who she is. She started writing earlier this year and hasn't stopped since, including participating in spoken word events and now being published in *Words By*. A lot of Jasmine's poetry stems from societal issues and empowering women. She focuses on how altered perceptions can influence change. *"My motivation in writing is to encourage people my age to build up their confidence and seek something they enjoy and flourish in it. Because everyone has the talent and the capability to do so."*

Saara Mohammed *p.137*
Saara Mahomed was born and bought up in London, finding it very rewarding to be in the midst of such a diverse city. *"I have friends who come from all sorts of backgrounds and walks of life."* Saara's passions include reading, writing and keeping up with all the tech news as this forms part of her day job. She uses writing as a form of journal writing and usually writes in

the form of short poetry. You can read more of her poetry on Instagram @saaraisapoet.

Kate Lawrence *p.137*
Kate Lawrence was born in Newcastle-Upon-Tyne and moved to Sydney age nine. She now plays in Slagatha Christie, a Canberra based, three-piece band, with friends Jess and Stephen. Playing since May 2017, Slagatha Christie started from nothing and each member learned to play their instruments together. Since then, they've featured on national radio and toured four states. *"A real turning point was starting to see crowds singing our lyrics back to us. We realised people were listening."* Since then, they've been more thoughtful about the work they put out into the world. This excerpt is from their song Lionel, which is about those moments that remind us we don't really matter in the grand scheme of things; it's lonely, but it also kind of takes the pressure off.

Mithila aka India Maya *p.138*
India Maya, is an Indian-born, Australian writer. Moved by the absurdity of existence, her poetry reflects the paradoxes, conflicts, and compelling fortuities of human experience. Her poem *Abstracted Ambition* explores the distractions and destruction wrought by human greed. She invites the reader to contemplate how we, as individuals, and collectively, conceptualise freedom and our boundaries of control. View her collection of poetry and other upcoming creative projects on Instagram @artindiamaya.

Jamiu Agboke *p.139*
Jamiu Agboke (@syn_iii) was born in Nigeria and raised in the UK. Jamiu's culture is constantly shifting and evolving. It has no fixed address – especially in a city like London which gives birth to numerous hybrids of cultures. Jamiu is an artist and makes art to celebrate and explore what binds us all. *"Being human can sometimes feel like imprisonment. Like being caged in physical form, fettered by attachment. Yet, in this state lies a strange contradiction; I am at once aware of my humanness and powerless to transcend it, at once elevated and imprisoned by the palace of identity I have constructed around myself. Confined by my own attempts to answer the unyielding question: Who am I? In striving to transcend one's physical self, one becomes more bound to its constraints. A great deal of art has been made under the banner of the paradox, in no detriment to its potency. I seek to break down the internal programming that governs*

how we see ourselves. My intention is to connect intimately with the impulses that drive us to make statements about ourselves."

Kai Larasi aka Soloman The Wizard *p.140*
With innovative and creative wordplay, Soloman The Wizard is taking on the poetry and spoken word scene word by word and captivating audiences across the country. *"I've been grateful to see my poetry being commissioned to be featured on the Digital Visitors Guide at the Tower of London and now also here in the* Words By *book, which is an absolutely amazing project. Whether on the stage or on paper, my aim as a poet is to deliver incredibly powerful messages in order to walk in my Purpose - which is to spread Love."*

Lucrecia-Seline *p.142*
Lucrecia-Seline is a writer, poet, trustee of Poetic Unity and an advocate for mental health and sexual abuse. With her raw truths in performance poetry and writing she hopes to inspire, empower, and force change, as well as breaks societies comfortability with taboo subjects. Lucrecia-Seline is currently working on a project titled *B.O.N.D.A.G.E* aimed at removing the stigmas and stereotypes around rape/sexual abuse. She is also working on a second project titled *The Prettiest Episode You've Ever Seen* which is aimed at highlighting the daily struggles of four people with different diagnoses of a mental health illness and how it is sometimes not noticeable to the public eye. Lucrecia-Seline is extremely passionate about the work she does (as she has personal experiences with these things and did not feel she had the help needed at the time). She hopes to be the voice for those unable to speak for themselves.

Chloe Kim *p.144*
Chloe Kim is the Co-Founder and former CEO of IYCPOP, a high growth food and beverage start-up in Australia. Presently a marketer for FMCG group, she is a LLB Law Graduate from the London School of Economics and Political Science. A strong believer in trying everything once, she is always seeking new experiences, lessons and skills while traveling around the world. Find her on Instagram @chloejaekim.

Katerina Nikita *p.144*
Katerina Nikita is an Athenian living the expat life as a Londoner in the making. She is flaneuse, trilingual, bibliophile and a multipassionate polymath.

Natural Wright *p.145*
Natural Wright is a spoken word artist, model and presenter, with a passion for community affairs and promotes self-empowerment and development. She burst into the spoken word world in late 2017 with her down-to-earth style of poetry. It is often raw but always emotive and engaging to her audiences. Her poetry often highlights the female perspective, but is also well received by the opposite sex. Natural works as a teacher; leading an alternative provision for learners with social, emotional and behavioural difficulties and has worked within the education sector for over 10 years. Growing up and living in London for the last four decades, her art is a reflection of the world she sees through her own eyes. As well as a popular poet, she is a model and hosts a talk show called NATURALIE on Heritage Television. Facebook: Natural 'Poetic' Wright, Instagram: @naturalie_poetic (poetry) or @naturalie_beautiful (modelling) and YouTube: Naturalie Poetic Wright.

Lams *p.148*
Lams is a spoken word poet, singer and natural story-teller who uses rhyme, rhythm and repetition along with her background in theatre and performing arts to powerfully deliver carefully thought out messages, leaving audiences emotional yet ready to reflect. She explores an array of topics from religion and political injustice to love and relationships, so her poetry and performance often takes readers and audience members through a rollercoaster of emotions. Find her on Instagram @olabara.

Erica-Renee Hassan-Sadiq *p.150*
Erica-Renee is 11-years-old and lives in East London. *"My passion is to take pictures when I'm out and about, dance and I really enjoying computer coding and editing."*

Sophie Mackenzie *p.152*
Sophie orders the chicken livers at Nandos... blaming a vivacious love for creativity and peculiarity for her strange life choices. Moving between Newcastle-Upon-Tyne, Sydney and Edinburgh, she now lives in East London, holding on to a unique Aussie-Geordie accent. *Wildflower* reflects on her time at university where she studied law whilst running club nights. It touches on the tension between an exciting new world and her commitment to human rights – and her attempts to find

meaning in each to overcome depression. After eight years, she fought the disease, and won. Sophie was recently awarded Young Humanitarian of the Year for extraordinary humanitarian service and is also one of the Co-Founders of Words By. Instagram: @snmackenzie.

Naomi Shimada *p.155*
Naomi Shimada is a model, host and writer. She was born in Japan and raised between Tokyo, the UK and the south of Spain. Naomi developed her platform speaking out against oppressive practices and unrealistic beauty standards in the fashion industry. Now she's trying to push the needle on conversations about humanity with the hopes of encouraging others to step out of their comfort zones. Instagram: @naomishimada.

Sylvanna Chance aka Sadface The Poet *p.155*
Sylvanna Chance aka Sadface The Poet (@SadfaceThePoet) is a self-proclaimed jack of all trades, master of none, from Luton. Sylvanna is also an improv poet, writer and performer who's work mainly speaks on identity in the changing landscape of today. She is currently working on six different events to raise Lutons profile and allow it to take part in the bidding for City of Culture.

Bre Graham *p.156*
Bre Graham is a writer and editor. She has been published in Harper's Bazaar, The Guardian, Dazed, Riposte, Stylist and more, where she writes about food, travel and culture. She has also had poetry published by the New River Press, was Associate Editor at Oh Comely for two years and has written recipes series for Rachel Khoo's website and Refinery29. Originally from Sydney, she grew up in Singapore and now lives and works in London. Bre is currently writing her first book of stories and recipes.

Adannay *p.158*
23-year-old singer-songwriter Adannay has been passionate about music from a young age. Drawing inspiration from the likes of Jill Scott, Emily King and Luther Vandross, she uses vocal harmony and lyricism to tell stories. However, as a black woman identifying as queer, she seldom discovered music that spoke to her own experiences of moving through the world. Adannay channels those feelings of 'otherness' into her song writing, narrating from lesser-heard perspectives,

sometimes but not always inspired by personal experience. *Wake Up Call* is a spoken word piece that inspired the intro to Adannays debut EP. Find *Wake Up Call* and more music by Adannay on Spotify and all major music platforms. Follow Adannay on Instagram @Adannay.music. Enquiries to adannay.music@gmail.com.

Chloe Pearson *p.159*
Chloe Pearson is a poet from Derbyshire living London. Writing in the style of punk poetry, taking inspiration from Britain's forgotten villages, the climate crisis, what it means to be a man, love, death and sex.

Sandy Aziz *p.162*
Sandy Aziz is a fashion addict dedicated to advocating a lifestyle laced with adventure, integrity and creativity. By trade, a lawyer, she is always an avid believer in education, with a Bachelor of Arts in English Literature from the UT Austin, JD and MBA from Texas Tech University. *"Each of us can and should strive to 'become' the best version of ourselves rather than just exist in 'being'."*

Chevonesse Smith *p.160*
Chevonesse Smith is a Jamaican born poet, raised in the UK. She is a chef by profession but enjoys the creative arts and likes to write poetry and create music in her spare time. She started writing at a young age as a way to process and reflect on her emotions after the passing of her mother. She sees poetry as a way for her to connect with the world around her and hopes her poetry will inspire the younger generation to be more accepting of their emotions, whilst understanding the importance of self-expression.

Rebecca Close *p.162*
Rebecca Close is an artist, poet and translator. Her collection *valid, virtual, vegetable reality* was chosen by Vahni Capildeo to win the Melita Hume Prize. She has a collaborative practice with Anyely Marín Cisneros, whose work bridges antiracism in contemporary art and science practices, new media and feminist epistemologies and poetics. Their research often culminates in performative interventions that combine collective reading of poetic-political texts with multimedia elements, as well as the creation of workshops and research groups.

Georgina Cundell *p.159*
Georgina, 23, lives in the heart of Manchester city centre, where she has immersed herself in since moving as a student six years ago. Georgina was blessed with a wonderful childhood, growing up in a village in the beautiful Yorkshire Dales, *"a place I definitely still call home."* She cares for every living being there is, including the beautiful, wonderful, frustrating and complex world we live in, whilst she unapologetically wears her heart on her sleeve.

Ajay Singh *p.163*
Ajay Singh is studying social work and has a dream to create a football academy for homeless people. A qualified social worker graduated from University of Kent, as an A26 scholar, Ajay is now starting work in children in care team in Kent County Council.

Constantinos Kyriacou aka Mindful Poet *p.164*
Constantinos' motivation for writing poetry has stemmed from their experiences of life and battling with their own mental health. They use poetry as a form of therapy. Their poetry is a collection of thoughts from an anxious mind (their own). Although based on their own experiences, they have no doubt that their poems are relatable. Their hope is that, through their poetry; they can let people know it's okay not to be okay all the time. We all have our down days. We all have anxieties in one form or another. Constantinos hopes to spark a conversation about mental health, and save a life, simply by opening-up and talking. *"It's time that we put the stereotypes and preconceptions of mental health that so many people unfortunately still hold, to bed."*

Luana Do Rosario Nicolau *p.166*
Luana tends to go by Lua, Luna, or Moonchild and is a mix of races: Portuguese, Cape Verdean and Angolese. *"I write. I teach. I care. I write to remain sane in a world where everything is designed to drive you insane. I was put on this earth to be heard."* Luana recently got back from Cambodia where she was teaching English to children and young adults. Whilst out there she also travelled around the country and lived amongst Khmer people to gain a further understanding about what real life is actually about. Luana may still be young but her life has not been short lived, *"I have travelled far and wide in these young years. I want to inspire, I want to challenge, I want to see growth. I want to LIVE in a world where people merely exist."*

James Jones *p.168*
James Jones is an award-winning British director who makes documentary films for international television and theatrical release.

Maryam Chaudhri *p.170*
Maryam Chaudhri, 20, lives in London and graduated Kings College London with a BA in History. With heritage from both Pakistan and India, Maryam writes about what identity means to her and other people.

Hussain Manawer *p.171*
Between the grit of East London and the charisma of Essex, sits the unassuming town named Ilford, home to the iconic Ilford Lane, Belgrave Road and internationally recognised poet, Hussain Manawer. Having been inspired by a school teacher who urged him to enter a poetry competition, on his return to school from exclusion, fast forward a decade or so and Hussain Manawer now travels across the world to deliver raw performances that pack an emotional and inspiring punch. Having supported the likes of Cher and Ed Sheeran and spoken along-side world leaders such as HRH Meghan Markle and actress Emma Watson, it was the many nights spent in his garden shed and attic bedroom where Hussain began to perfect his craft. Using poetry as a tool to allow communities to understand societal issues from various standpoints, Hussain was awarded The Points of Lights award, from 10 Downing Street, for his work in mental health shortly after setting the Guinness World Record, for The World's Largest Mental Health Lesson. He is also a London 2012 Olympic Torchbearer whilst being Kings College London's youngest Honorary Fellow and the youngest Doctorate of Arts from Oxford Brooke's University.

Mazin Ali *p.171*
Mazin is from Sudan and has been in the UK since 2015. He likes football and helping other people. Passionate about being part of the community in the UK, he likes the hospitality of people in the UK. He is, simply, a happy person.

Abdulla Mansour aka Softspoken *p.172*
Abdulla is a full-time science teacher, amateur performance poet, husband, son, brother, Londoner, Iraqi and ardent Manchester United fan (support your local team people). He goes by @softspoken3aboud on Instagram. He started writing in response to the

Christchurch shootings and it unleashed a passion for writing he never knew he had. Having attended spoken word events on and off for two years, it was through the constant pressure of PoetCurious and Prestige Karlla that he eventually decided to give it a try myself. Abdulla is a former asylum seeker who is dismayed by the lack of compassion recent refugees have been treated by the media and the current government. *"My family arrived by plane. That people need to risk their lives for the same chance now is heart breaking, cruel and ultimately avoidable. Empathy is not rare: it only seems like it because people are afraid to speak out. Don't be."*

Washington Ali *p.174*
Washington has lived a multi-faceted life, experiencing home, private and state education. With these contrasting environments he could not comprehend what 'this' (being life) was about and caused a surge of curiosity. This led him to travel the globe, create music, learn spiritual practices, invest in property and co-found a tech company. These experiences have allowed him to discover his purpose, which he believes it to be of service to people whether be it empowering people or just a smile in the street.

Siti Aisah *p.175*
Siti is a migrant from Indonesia and has lived in London for nearly four years. She studies health and social care in London. She loves to cook and learn how to become a good person. She also loves to read Indonesian books. She hopes she can make people's life better. She loves the UK because she can meet many people from different cultures, backgrounds and experiences.

Greta Bellamacina *p.176*
Greta Bellamacina is a poet, actress and filmmaker. She was born in London and trained at RADA before doing a BA in English at King's College London. Her work has been praised internationally, with the ability to bring a contemporary poetic sensibility to her chosen art form. Her latest books include *Smear for Girls* and *Selected Poems 2015-2017* which is currently being translated into Spanish, both books are published with New River Press.

Tahmina Begum *p.177*
Tahmina Begum is based between London and Birmingham and lives by the hashtag #badandbengali. Working as an editor and journalist for the past eight years and with recent bylines in I-D, Dazed, AnOther, HuffPost UK, Man Repeller, Metro, gal-dem and more, Begum is also CEO and EIC of the print publication and platform XXY Magazine and columnist at Screen Shot magazine. She has recently contributed to *Comfort Zones*, a collection of essays in aid of Women For Women UK, writing about second-generation guilt and ease and *Mixed Feelings*, a collection of essays about our complicated relationship with social media. Her work focuses on culture, communities and connection.

Orin Begum *p.180*
Orin is a corporate finance lawyer working for an international law firm in London. She stumbled into poetry during her final year of reading law at the University of Oxford, as a way to address her experiences of being a South Asian Muslim woman in a predominately white, middle class university. Her poetry is inspired by the struggles and strength of South Asian women, her experiences with colourism and body shaming and the complications of growing up as a 1.5 generation immigrant living in a council estate in East London. She goes by the handle @poetrie_by_oreenie on Instagram.

Jamel Rust *p.183*
Jamel believes everyone has a story to tell. Born in London, raised in New York, the son of Jamaican immigrants and conversant in Mandarin Chinese as a result of years of volunteer work in the Mandarin speaking community, has left him with a unique perspective on home, identity, and culture. Jamel was first introduced to poetry at the age of 11 by a 6th grade elementary teacher who saw beyond the disruptive student, to the future leader that his words would allow him to be. He has shared his poetic stories at historic venues such as the Nuroyican Poet's Café, and Bowery Poetry club and in front of the Mayor at the New York City Board of Education. This led to an appearance on the NBC Good Morning Today show, the Hillingdon Literary Festival in London, and several other talent showcases. @Justamanexpressinglove is not just a stage name, persona or facade - it's an ethos, it is a standard he tries to live his life by. *"My poetry conveys optimism and anxieties, confidence yet vulnerability."*

Tarik Clavier *p.184*
Tarik has been practicing poetry since 2018. He has a strong faith in his religion, a logical mind and a creative heart, which he uses to enjoy dissecting the world around him. He uses his knowledge of music to play with pace and rhythm in his poems. Being a mixed-race youth raised in Hackney, a melting pot of different cultures, Tarik understood the value of uniqueness very early on; a theme of the power of an individual permeates most of his works. By 16, he was organising high-profile charity fundraisers and distributions to the homeless, amongst other volunteer work. After five years of this, it became apparent that everyone has unique battles and perspectives on everything, which shouldn't go to waste in a crowd mentality. Henceforth, Tarik aims for his works to act as catalysts for unique and original thought.

Rhys Lewis *p.186*
Crafting his songs with a maturity that belies his years, Rhys Lewis has consistently showcased his talent for songwriting, and as a result his music continues to reach an ever-growing global fanbase. Originally from Oxford, the 27-year-old singer-songwriter has now toured the world extensively from the UK to Asia and EU to US, playing electrifying headline shows that draw fans that queue overnight to be first in line, alongside playing festivals such as SXSW. His music has featured on hit TV shows and has garnered fans in peers such as Julia Michaels, Sigrid and Lewis Capaldi. His debut album, both co-written and produced by him, is out in early 2020.

Amy Basil *p.188*
Amy Basil is an executive in the film and television industry as well as a writer of creative non-fiction and poetry. She lives in South London with her partner, Joshua, a documentary filmmaker and journalist.

Omar Alfrouh *p.192*
Omar is a Syrian refugee and has been in the UK since 2017. What makes him happy is being in society and taking every chance in front of him. His dream is to be a brain surgeon.

Peter deGraft-Johnson aka The Repeat Beat Poet *p.194*
The Repeat Beat Poet is a broadcaster, journalist and Hip Hop poet who fuses traditional poetics and Hip Hop culture to capture and extend moments of time, thought and feeling. The Repeat Beat Poet has appeared across the UK and internationally, in musical, theatrical, and poetic performances at venues such as The Royal Albert Hall, Battersea Arts Centre, Ronnie Scott's Jazz Club, and at multiple festivals including the Edinburgh Fringe and Brainchild. He has facilitated poetry workshops in the medical and educational sectors, produced and hosts the monthly spoken word events Boomerang and Pen-Ting, is a house emcee with Hip Hop label and jam night Imaginary Millions, and is the creator of the Hip Hop/spoken Word radio show #TheRepeatBeatBroadcast. In 2019, he was nominated for a Jerwood Compton Poetry Fellowship.

Benny Bruce *p.195*
Benny Bruce is a spoken word poet from Croydon, South London. Benny aims to highlight societal issues and personal stories through wordplay whilst simultaneously inspiring and encouraging listeners. By painting pictures with words, and visions with verses, Benny is a spoken word poet who is looking to make a difference. Instagram & Twitter: @mistabruce_ and Youtube: Benny Bruce.

Kavita Puri *p.198*
Kavita Puri is a journalist and author of *Partition Voices; Untold British Stories.*

Nomusa Okorie *p.200*
Nomusa is a London born poet and spoken word artist. They are also studying Journalism at Coventry University.

Simon Anderson *p.201*
Simon Anderson is from Narrabeen, Sydney and is passionate about God and living humanely. Simon suffered from depression and hypomania in his teenage years, leading to an escape mechanism that includes writing poetry. Simon writes because *"written words can speak the contents of my heart better than spoken ones."*

Tommy Evans *p.202*
Hailing from a family of artists, innovation, imagination and industry are embedded in Tommy Evans' DNA. As a pioneering UK Hip Hop musician, Tommy has appeared on over forty releases; managed the influential YNR record label; collaborated

with multi-platinum and underground artists alike including Neneh Cherry, Foreign Beggars, Nutty P and Doc Brown to name a few. Tommy's music has been playlisted on Radio 1 and featured on MTV, Soccer AM, Inbetweeners and Kidulthood. More recently, Tommy Evans has made a name for himself as a published writer, spoken word artist and filmmaker earning a PhD in the process. Tommy's artistry has been praised by Stormzy, Dave, Example, Loyle Carner, Ghetts, Easy Mo Bee (producer of 2Pac and Notorious B.I.G.), Quincy (son of Diddy), No Malice (Clipse), Maverick Sabre, Mr Hudson, Andrez Harriott (Damage), Natalie Stewart (Floetry), Jammer, Jamal Edwards MBE and many more! This autumn, (Dr) Tommy Evans releases the LP Antifragile, an ambitious adaptation of his book Medusa Wore A Weave (Or In The Absence Of Magic) produced entirely by soulful beat-maker DJ Agent M. Brace for impact.

Elan Weedon aka EJ p.205

EJ is an actor and poet who grew up in Slough, England. He started writing to process the strange world around him. EJ has a mother who emigrated from St Vincent, and a father who was raised in Oxford by English and German parents (who met during the second world war). Therefore, the ideas of belonging and other, constant and change, are a regular theme in his work. Now as a 'middle class' mixed race millennial male in Britain, EJ uses poetry to question the answers he thought he had.

Sadie Davidson p.208

Sadie Davidson is a multi-slam winning performance poet, playwright, and author of two poetry collections, Tales From The Estate and The Poverty Guide Handbook. She has won the Kent Poetry Championship twice, been a Hammer & Tongue National finalist, and was a U.K Slam Championship semi-finalist for two years in a row. "All pretty unlikely considering I am also a recovering addict and former stripper who has experienced homelessness, domestic violence and poverty first hand – but poetry changed my life entirely. I now write extensively about my experiences to raise awareness of these issues, and my focus is on sharing the reality of lower working class life with as wide an audience as possible. I now offer a variety of poetry writing workshops for those who have been in similar situations, in the hope that writing might change their lives for the better as well." You can find more details at www.sadiedavidsonpoet.com. Instagram @sadiedpoet. Facebook: Sadie Davidson – Poet.

Nathan Henville p.210

Nathan has an Afro-Caribbean background; he has grown up in various areas in the South of England since he entered the care system. This allowed his personality to develop and heavily influenced his outlooks, aspirations and everyday morals. Nathan has since worked with charities such as Coram Voice, using his experience of the care system to learn and practice the importance of caring for vulnerable young people. Nathan takes a unique approach in being creative with his insights of life; having no trouble challenging the normal constructs of society. This has built a huge part of who he is today; previously using it in written work to reflect a system that is spoken so little about. He currently studies at a university in London whilst working part time and reflects on his own sociological perspectives by writing poetry. He hopes to produce a level of unified empathy.

Ally Thorn p.210

Ally Thorn is a young Australian artist carving her music career in London. A mix of RnB, Pop and Soul, her style has been compared to that of Tori Kelly and Jorja Smith. For Ally, music has been a life-long outlet for her struggles with self-doubt, anxiety and depression - as well as health problems, such as Polycystic Ovaries Syndrome. By crafting melodies and stories that speak to personal struggles, yet pedal messages of self-empowerment, Ally hopes that her art will resonate with those who may be suffering silently. Ally is set to release her most recent EP later this year. Having worked with ARIA award-winning producers and mentors such as Stuart Stuart, John Castle and Karen Jacobsen, Ally is keen to continue using her platform to raise awareness and open the conversation on mental health.

Remington Lavai p.211

Remington Lavai is a 27-year-old from East London, Hackney, with a Sierra Leonean, Nigerian and Congolese background. He started writing poetry at the age of 17 but was too scared to publicise his work because he felt it wasn't good enough. He started writing poetry because he loved English Literature at school. "So being able to write four lines with rhythm, word play and intellect was an amazing feeling for me." Similar to most London youth, Remington has gone through depression, family issues, environmental and social challenges, and more. *"In late 2018 and early 2019 I went through the lowest point in my life where I wanted to commit suicide. Overcoming that period in my life, I started writing spoken word about the good and bad situations we all face in today's society like depression, colourism, relationships and of course, great highlights I may have achieved."* Being able to write and meet people from every walk of life that can relate and enjoy his work is the reason he writes. Find him @sincerely_remington, and AY, who co-wrote White T-Shirt, a_yofficial.

Shamaila Jahangir *p.212*
Shamaila Jahangir is a 23-year-old based in North West London. Being in the educational field, she feels fortunate to have worked with children who come from different cultures, race, religion and class. Her poem embodies thoughts that she embeds in children, which is simply to take lead and become composers of their destiny without compromising their identity. *"The only thing we all share, despite differences and obstacles, is time. Value your time, use it wisely, as what you do with it will make the difference."* Follow her on Instagram @shamaillaa.

Ellie Scott *p.213*
Ellie Scott, 18, spent the majority of her growing years moving around a lot, across various towns in England. Ellie's writing helps validate her emotions and stays a constant in her world. Ellie writes not only to produce a creative outlet, but also to give herself access to the community that writing poetry comes with.

Lynn Enright *p.214*
Lynn Enright is an Irish writer and editor. She published her first book *Vagina: A Re-Education* in spring 2019 and she writes about health, sex, feminism, politics, pop culture and most other topics for a variety of publications including the Guardian, The Irish Times, Vogue, Elle, Grazia and Refinery29. She lives in East London.

Oliver (OT) Wells *p.216*
OT Wells is a 19-year-old writer and philosopher from the UK Find his blog at www.eternalkeyhole.wordpress.com.

Special Thanks

Words By was a passion project driven by the generosity of others.

Words and Stories - Contributors
To the contributors who donated their words and stories, thank you.
You are all forces of change.

Project Partnership - Unicef Next Generation London
Unicef Next Generation London is a community of young professionals in London who donate their time and skills on behalf of Unicef. Next Gen incubates creative and unique ideas to fundraise and advocate for Unicef, and works across all industry sectors to raise awareness and educate our community.

Design - Charlie Smith Design
Charlie Smith Design were able to bring our brand to life from the very first conversation. Charlie Smith Design combines a passion for design with straight speaking strategy to create thoughtful and engaging solutions, which have continued to serve Words By since 2018.

Font – Steensen Varming
Use of the Varming typeface (created by Søren Varming of Punktum Design and Henrik Kubel of A2-TYPE) granted by Steensen Varming, an engineering design consultancy exclusively focused on doing good work with good people for good reasons.

Website – Benedict Silva
Benedict Silva is an incredible freelance website designer and developer who can be contacted via talk@bendesilva.com.

Social and Creative Lead - Alexandra (Ali) Dowton
Following a career path in marketing and communications, Ali's appreciation for creative arts intensified since moving from North Queensland, Australia to London. Ali brought a unique style and strong identity to the Words By brand, and continues to do so, one post at a time!

Sponsorship – Anonymous
Thank you to the anonymous donor who generously supported this project and covered the costs of our first print run with CPI Colour.

Support with outreach
Amy Spiller and the Young Citizens of Coram
Catrin Nye of BBC
Fisky of Mind Over Matter
Miss Yankey of Poetry Prescribed
Emily Ames of Sonder & Tell
Serena Guen of SUITCASE Magazine
Monica Tanouye and Victoria Roe of Unicef UK

Co-Founders of Words By

Sophie Mackenzie
Sophie Mackenzie has worked in a variety of humanitarian contexts across Africa, Asia, Australia and Europe, placing a strong emphasis on grass-root collaboration. She has supported some of the world's most vulnerable groups, such as ex-child soldiers and trafficking victims. Sophie graduated from the University of Edinburgh, where she studied an MA Law and International Relations (Hons) with her Masters focusing on sex trafficking, asylum and refugee law. Sophie now works for the British Red Cross, focusing on emergency appeals and strategic fundraising projects. In 2019, she was awarded the Red Cross' Young Humanitarian of the Year. Sophie often travels to refugee camps across Europe to offer legal aid. It was in Baobab Camp, Rome, where she was originally inspired to create Words By as refugees gifted her poems as thank yous.

"The goal for Words By was to create a platform that strips away negative white noise and see humans as humans no matter their background. We wanted to create a book so beautiful, raw, reactive and inclusive that it acts as a stunning record of our times - one that celebrates our similarities and finds beauty in our differences."

Bethany Grace Gill
A lover of all things people and planet, Bethany Gill was part of the duo (alongside Sophie) that imagined this project and brought it to life. With a passion for words, Bethany graduated from the University of Edinburgh after studying English Literature and Creative Writing, where she wrote plays and poems as part of her degree. Bethany has a rooted understanding of building grass-root communities in London, with years of experience as a Community Manager specialising in new businesses, volunteer projects and start-ups.

"We're not just creating a poetry book, we're telling a story, we are bringing people together. Words by is a project close to all our hearts and I'm thrilled to be working with such a great team. I can't wait to see what the world thinks of it and where it goes next!"

Noura Al-Maashouq
Noura Al-Maashouq graduated from Georgetown University and went on to earn a Masters degree from the Courtauld Institute of Art. Upon graduation, she worked in a contemporary art gallery in London and became involved with Unicef Next Generation London, eventually taking on the role of Chair. Having grown up between the Philippines, Saudi Arabia, and the US, Noura recognizes the importance of Unicef's global reach and believes it is our universal responsibility to support these efforts. She was drawn to Next Gen by its engagement with young professionals across all sectors who lend their skills, time and resources to advocate on behalf of the world's most vulnerable children. Noura believes we should never stop educating ourselves and others on humanitarian issues, and recognizes the many ways local efforts can support global issues.

To join the team or for more information, email wordsbyuk@gmail.com or follow us on Instagram @wordsby___

UNICEF

About Unicef Next Generation London

Unicef Next Generation London is a community of young professionals in London who donate their time and skills on behalf of Unicef. Next Gen incubates creative and unique ideas to fundraise and advocate for Unicef and works across all industry sectors to raise awareness and educate our community.

Unicef Next Generation has raised over £3 million through international campaigns like #CookForSyria, Migrate and Words By, and through a variety of innovative partnerships, events and philanthropy.

Next Gen brings together a community committed to helping transform the lives of the world's most vulnerable children. To become a part of the Next Gen community email info@nextgenlondon.com or visit www.nextgenlondon.com.

About Unicef

Unicef is the world's leading organisation for children. Founded by the United Nations in the aftermath of World War Two, Unicef has been helping to create a better world for children in more than 190 countries for over 70 years.

Unicef ensures more of the world's children are fed, vaccinated, educated and protected than any other organisation. They have done more to influence laws, policies and customs to help protect children than anyone else in history. They get things done. And they're not going to stop until the world is a safe place for all our children.

The Children's Emergency Fund

Thank you - by purchasing a copy of Words By, you are supporting the Children's Emergency Fund and helping Unicef reach children in danger. This means Unicef is able to provide life-saving food, clean water, vaccines and health care for children in emergencies, as well as education and protection from violence, exploitation and abuse.

This is especially important, as situations like climate change and violent conflict continue to force children to flee their homes and become an internally displaced person (IDPs), refugee or migrant. Whether alone or with family members, these children are increasingly facing higher fences, stricter border control and regular push-backs.

Now you've finished reading, follow us!

This book may be finished, but our story continues on Instagram @wordsby___ (that's four underscores). We will continue to share the stories of refugees and other human beings who have been impacted by social injustice, whilst celebrating words that bind us together. Watch our #WordsBy_ community grow and stay connected with updates on future events and more exciting projects to come. And don't forget to #WordsBy_ so we can keep up to date with your progress too!

Published in 2019 by SUITCASE Media International Ltd.
Designed by Charlie Smith Design Ltd.
Edited by Sophie Mackenzie, Bethany Gill and Noura Al-Maashouq.
Printed and bound in London by CPI Colour.
Varming Font by Steensen Varming with Søren Varming of
Punktum Design and Henrik Kubel of A2-TYPE.

Disclaimer
The facts and opinions expressed in this publication are solely the
opinions of the respective authors/photographers and do not necessarily
reflect the views of Unicef Next Generation London or Unicef UK.

All profits from this book will help support all children in danger through
Unicef's Next Generation. All text, photography & design 100% donated.

WORDS BY____

www.wordsby.co.uk
◎ @wordsby___